W9-BXY-270

ANGER AND ADDICTION: BREAKING THE RELAPSE CYCLE

Anger and Addiction: Breaking the Relapse Cycle

A Teaching Guide for Professionals

JO CLANCY, LMSW-ACP, LCDC

PSYCHOSOCIAL PRESS
MADISON, CONNECTICUT

Library of Congress Cataloging-in-Publication Data

Clancy, Jo.
Anger and addiction : Breaking the relapse cycle : a teaching guide for professionals / Jo Clancy.
p. cm.
Includes bibliographical references.
ISBN 1-887841-02-4
1. Social case work with alcoholics—United States.
2. Alcoholism—Treatment—United States. 3. Anger. I. Title.
HV5279.C58 1996
362.29'286—dc20 96-7939
CIP

Manufactured in the United States of America

Contents

Preface

This text represents 6 years of clinical social work practice with recovering alcoholics. During the course of my interventions, I observed a pattern of relapse that appeared to correlate with clients' inability to constructively express their feelings without first using mind-altering substances to reduce inhibitions. I noted that some clients appeared outwardly hostile and defensive. Others elected to boil silently inside. Despite the dramatic difference in presentation, both types of clients experienced a precariously high relapse potential. Their lack of awareness and of adequate coping skills impeded their progress in traditional recovery programs, prompting me to develop an alternative intervention program to address both issues simultaneously.

This book is an effort to share knowledge acquired during my ongoing journey with these clients. Materials drawn from the sources noted fostered the creation of intervention strategies, which were modified continuously, as my clients and my experience working with this population dictated. This is an intervention model that I practice as well as teach, and it works! My goal is to guide practitioners in their efforts to provide clients with the greatest opportunity to achieve long-term, quality sobriety, i.e., the difference between being dry (not drinking/using) and sober (not drinking/using, coupled with the acquisition and application of more productive ways of thinking and behaving). I hope the information presented stimulates your thinking and provides new ideas for working with addicted populations.

Acknowledgments

To Jay Sonkin, Ph.D., and Michael Durphy, M.D., whose 1985 edition of *Learning to Live without Violence: A Handbook for Men* served as a primary resource for this book. My thanks also to Ms. Jeanne Deschner, whose 1984 publication *The Hitting Habit: Anger Control for Battering Couples* provided additional inspiration and technical skills for Part 2 of my intervention program. I am also indebted to the work of Dr. Albert Ellis, whose theoretical framework guided my work, and to Dr. Gerald Corey, who presented an excellent overview and comparison of the major theoretical perspectives currently guiding clinical practice in his 1991 text, *Theory and Practice of Counseling and Psychotherapy* (4th ed.). Thanks also to Kevin Grillo, Bill Crabtree, and Travis Courville, whose tireless efforts to make me computer literate advanced the progress of this book. A second, very special thanks to Bill Crabtree. He patiently adjusted my computer programs, removing glitches I created during my writing adventure (and there were *many*!).

On a more personal level, to my husband Vinny and my two older sons, Albin and Sean, who tolerated my creative mood swings and struggles to master the computer. Their encouragement gave me the courage to pursue my dream. To my baby son, Vincent, whose premature birth provided me with 6 months off to complete the first draft of this book, and to my mother and sister, who provided inspiration when I needed it most. I also applaud the hundreds of clients who trusted me enough to share their feelings and risk trying new thoughts and behaviors. Without their guidance, the anger management-relapse prevention program would never have been born.

Part 1

The Identification Process

FOCUS: Early identification of stimuli that elicit anger and substance abuse, so that appropriate coping skills can be developed and implemented

1

Defining Anger and Addiction

Setting the Stage

What is anger and how does it affect the relapse cycle? Attempts to answer this question raise a second, equally complex issue. Once anger is defined and the dynamics that fuel this interaction identified, what theoretical framework can provide interventions most likely to produce positive outcomes for clients? These questions will be the focus of this chapter.

The literature is filled with definitions of anger. Several researchers (Fonberg, 1979; MaClean, 1955; Moyer, 1976; Schachter, 1957) hypothesize that anger is a mixture of fear and pain and that response choices are heavily influenced by individuals' perceptions of specific events. Schachter (1971), along with Green and Green (1979), likened anger to a computer program that mobilizes the body to carry out predetermined operations. Spielberger, Jacobs, Russell, and Crane (1983) provide a more comprehensive approach, defining anger as an immediate emotional state that can range from mild irritation to rage. They expand this definition by delineating subtypes of anger: (1) aggression, an actual behavior intended to harm another; (2) hostility, an attitude toward a specific person or the world; (3) resentment, a process in which anger is stored; and (4) hatred, the end product of resentment. Williams and

Williams (1993) assume a similar position, defining anger as an emotional state influenced by personal expectations, often unrealistic in nature, that generate reactions from minor irritation to aggressive behavioral acts. I view anger as a combination of biopsychosocial factors whose interaction leads to a highly variable pattern of response choices. Further discussion of this approach will follow in Chapters 2 and 3.

The literature is equally diverse in defining addiction. Prior to 1960, addiction was viewed primarily as an issue of morality. The work of Dr. Jellinek (1960) led to a dramatic redefinition process, and addiction was recognized as a disease by the American Medical Association. The work of Leiber, Hasumara, Teschke, Matsuzaki, and Korsten (1975), Milam and Ketcham (1981), and Schuckit, Li, Cloninger, and Deitrich (1985) furthered the concept of addiction as a primary disease. They postulated that some people are born with differences in brain chemistry, increasing the potential for addictive disease. Nathan, Titler, Lowenstein, Solomon, and Rossi (1970) and Mello (1972) expanded this definition, identifying addiction as a condition influenced by genetic factors and reinforced by individuals' beliefs and expectations about the effect substances might produce. Vaillant (1983) referred to addiction as an essential disease similar to hypertension. He postulated that medical treatment alone was insufficient, and recommended early detection as a means of initiating changes in thoughts, feelings, attitudes, and lifestyle necessary to control the disease process. In 1986, Gorski and Miller defined addiction as a physical disease that produces long-term physical, psychological, and social damage; they referred to addiction as a biopsychosocial disease. My beliefs are parallel to the work Gorski and Miller initiated and continue to explore and develop.

The preceding definitions influenced my thinking as I began to monitor the interaction between anger and addiction in my chronically relapsing clients. A cluster of qualities emerged as critical factors in the activation of the anger-relapse cycle.

1. *Biological determinants.* Anger and addiction each generate specific, involuntary physiological reactions that occur in response to internal and external stimuli. These reactions have a biological basis and are not under conscious control.
2. *Environmental determinants.* External factors play a critical role in shaping individuals' response choices. Learning to recognize

personal risk factors increases opportunities for application of productive alternatives.

3. *Warning signs*. Anger and addiction each produce signals alerting individuals that emotional reactiveness and/or relapse are imminent. These signals create minute shifts in physiological, cognitive, and behavioral reactions, which, when recognized, provide a framework for an alternative response.
4. *Dynamics of reinforcement.* The temporary relief produced by impulsive expressions of anger and substance abuse reinforce existing patterns of behavior. Since long-term negative consequences are generally delayed, interruption of this cycle poses a significant challenge during treatment.
5. *Intervening variables*. Anger and addiction are both influenced by past experiences, interpretation of current events, and the effectiveness of existing responses. A negative frame of reference, faulty perceptual set, and/or a lack of consequences for existing unproductive responses seriously affect motivation to initiate change.
6. *Recurrent patterns of behavior*. Anger and addiction are both cyclical in nature. As tension increases, a cycle of reaction-frustration-reaction occurs, exacerbating levels of distress. Episodes of anger dyscontrol or substance abuse occur with increasing frequency as individuals attempt to diminish unpleasant reactions. Tension continues to escalate unless the cycle is interrupted.
7. *Response choices*. Although initial physiological reactions are beyond conscious control, awareness of their existence influences response choices. With training, individuals can learn to identify reactions and develop a repertoire of thoughts, feelings, and behaviors to redefine response choices.
8. *Potential for negative consequences*. Anger and addiction, over time, generate significant, negative personal consequences. Failure to identify and redirect faulty response choices adversely affects health, mental health, employment, relationships, and self-esteem.
9. *Aggregate repercussions*. Anger and addiction potentiate each other's negative effects. The synergistic reaction generated by combining these variables significantly increases the risk of devastating negative consequences.
10. *Potential for change*. Once individuals are taught to recognize triggers and cues precipitating anger dyscontrol and/or substance

abuse, development and application of coping skills to modify faulty thoughts, feelings, and behavior becomes possible.

Defining anger, addiction, and the synergistic creation of an anger-relapse cycle leads us to a second question, posed in the first paragraph of this chapter: What theoretical framework can provide interventions most likely to produce positive outcomes for clients? The prodigious task of identifying such a framework was greatly advanced by surveying the excellent synopsis and comparison of major theoretical perspectives in Corey (1991), followed by a closer review of each theory that appeared potentially useful in the development of my intervention model.

I first considered person-centered therapy (Rogers, 1951; Rogers & Wood, 1974) since clients with addictive diseases present with poor self-esteem and an intense need for acceptance. Although this approach provides a framework for unconditional positive regard, it does not provide the directive, action-oriented strategies essential to break through denial and establish more productive patterns of thoughts, feelings, and behavior.

A behavioral approach was considered next (Bandura, 1969, 1971a, 1971b, 1974, 1977, 1986; Barlow, 1978; Bellack & Hersen, 1985; Thoresen & Coates, 1980), since the central focus is on modifying maladaptive patterns of behavior and replacing them with productive alternatives. Although behavior change is one facet of interrupting the anger-relapse cycle, behavior therapy fails to attend to the thoughts and feelings that underlie existing behaviors.

A review of rational-emotive (Beck, 1976, 1988; Beck, Rush, Shaw, & Emery, 1979; Ellis, 1973, 1985; Ellis & Becker, 1982; Ellis & Dryden, 1987; Ellis & Greiger, 1977; Ellis & Harper, 1975; Ellis, McInerney, DiGiuseppe, & Yeager, 1988; Ellis & Whiteley, 1979; Walen, DiGuiseppe, & Wessler, 1980; Wessler & Wessler, 1980) and related cognitive-behavioral therapies (Annis, 1986; Annis & Davis, 1987a, 1987b; Daley, 1988; Mahoney, 1974; Mahoney & Thoresen, 1974; Marlatt & Gordon, 1985; Meichenbaum, 1977) identified a wealth of ideas that seemed compatible with my objective of interrupting the anger-relapse cycle. Rational-emotive therapy and related cognitive-behavioral approaches provide interventions that address cognitive, emotional, and behavioral aspects of response choices.

Although embedded in rational-emotive and cognitive-behavioral models of intervention, my model incorporates the belief that awareness of past experiences and their influence on current feelings, thoughts, and behavior is critical to the successful application of any strategy designed to elicit lasting change—a belief in direct conflict with basic tenets of these approaches. This incongruence led me to explore a broader-based, eclectic model recently developed by Carlo DiClemente (1993). DiClemente and his colleagues developed a transtheoretical model positing that incompatible theoretical beliefs regarding the etiology of problems can be integrated when striving to elicit behavior change. This model further supports the premise that recovery occurs in stages that are sequential and ordinal; however, recovery often contains a cyclical component, whereby clients must repeat various stages before successfully achieving long-term change.

The transtheoretical model evolved as DiClemente and his colleagues searched for elements necessary to achieve successful modification of addictive behaviors. Their search led to the discovery that medical, marital, behavioral, cognitive, and emotional perspectives each had supporters, however, none of these perspectives adequately explained why some clients succeeded and others failed in their quest for sustained sobriety. The transtheoretical model validates the potential role each of these perspectives, either separately or jointly applied, has in the modification of addictive behaviors, however, goes further by postulating that intentional change (i.e., the client's readiness for change coupled with their current position in the stages and cycles of change) is the key ingredient in outcome determination.

The anger management-relapse prevention model presented in this book adheres to DiClemente's contention that opposing theoretical perspectives can be merged to generate lasting change in clients' feelings, cognitions, and behaviors (once they reach a critical point in the process of intentional change). In Stage 1 of my model, clients are assisted in identifying the determinants of anger and addiction and the impact of past experiences on their current response choices. Although clearly in opposition to tenets of rational-emotive and cognitive-behavioral approaches, I believe this foundation is critical to the successful acquisition and application of intervention strategies presented in Stage 2.

The second stage is more congruent with the philosophies of rational-emotive and cognitive-behavioral approaches. A variety of interventions designed to address patterns of faulty thinking and behaviors provide alternative response choices that can be used separately or in combination. Techniques can be tailored to address both the client's stage of recovery and individual response style.

Stage 3 addresses the need for ongoing application, evaluation, and modification of emotions, cognitions, behaviors, and the interventions selected to address maladaptive response choices. My belief is that former patterns cannot be erased; however, we can minimize their impact by developing strategies to reduce the potential of calling them into action. Much like minimizing one computer program to create available memory to run additional programs, a portion of the screen is still committed to the initial program but requires much less memory to maintain it. Similarly, old emotions, cognitions, and behaviors continue to exist in our coping repertoire and may resurface in times of crisis, but by minimizing their influence in everyday life the potential of arresting the anger-relapse cycle is greatly enhanced.

The anger management-relapse prevention program is a comprehensive, action-oriented approach designed to assist clients in developing a higher quality of sobriety. Through a process of awareness, education, application, and modification clients learn to release themselves from self-defeating patterns of feeling, thinking, and behaving. A description of this 12-session training series and aftercare program are the focus of the remaining chapters in this book.

2

Physical and Psychological Determinants of Anger and Addiction

Session 1 of the anger management-relapse prevention training program provides clients with an overview of the physical and psychological determinants of anger and addiction. The purpose of this session is to help clients identify factors that influence their response choices and to differentiate between factors that are amenable to change and those that are not. This process begins with a description of anger dynamics, followed by a discussion of physical and psychological influences specific to addictive disease. Finally, the concept of the synergistic impact of these variables is introduced, along with models illustrating high- and low-risk relapse potentials (Figures 1 and 2).

Anger is presented as a normal, healthy emotion that is, at times, expressed inappropriately (withheld or misdirected). A distinction is drawn between reactions (involuntary physiological changes) and responses (individual response choices that occur once initial reactions subside). This distinction sets the stage for assigning client responsibility for actions and consequences once they develop an awareness of triggers and cues (Chapter 4) and acquire a repertoire of coping skills to

Figure 1. Model 1: High risk for relapse.

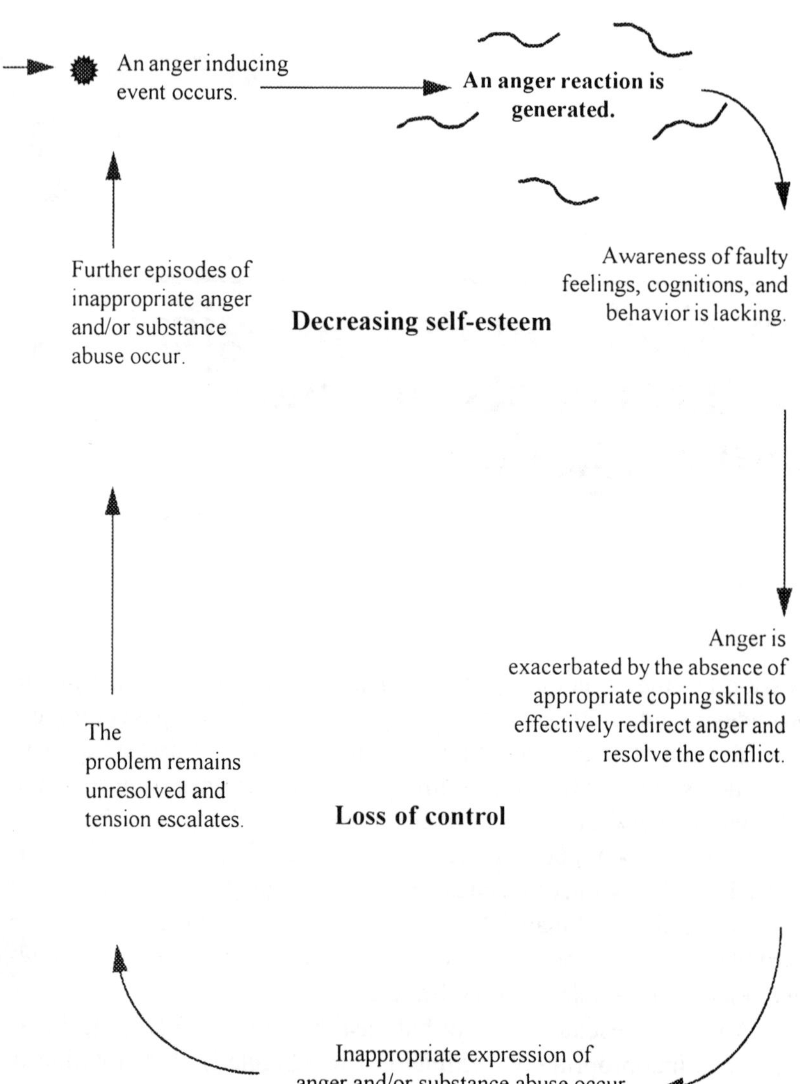

*The individual is trapped in a self-perpetuating cycle of negative response choices and has the perception that there is no avenue of escape.

Figure 2. Model 2: Low risk for relapse.

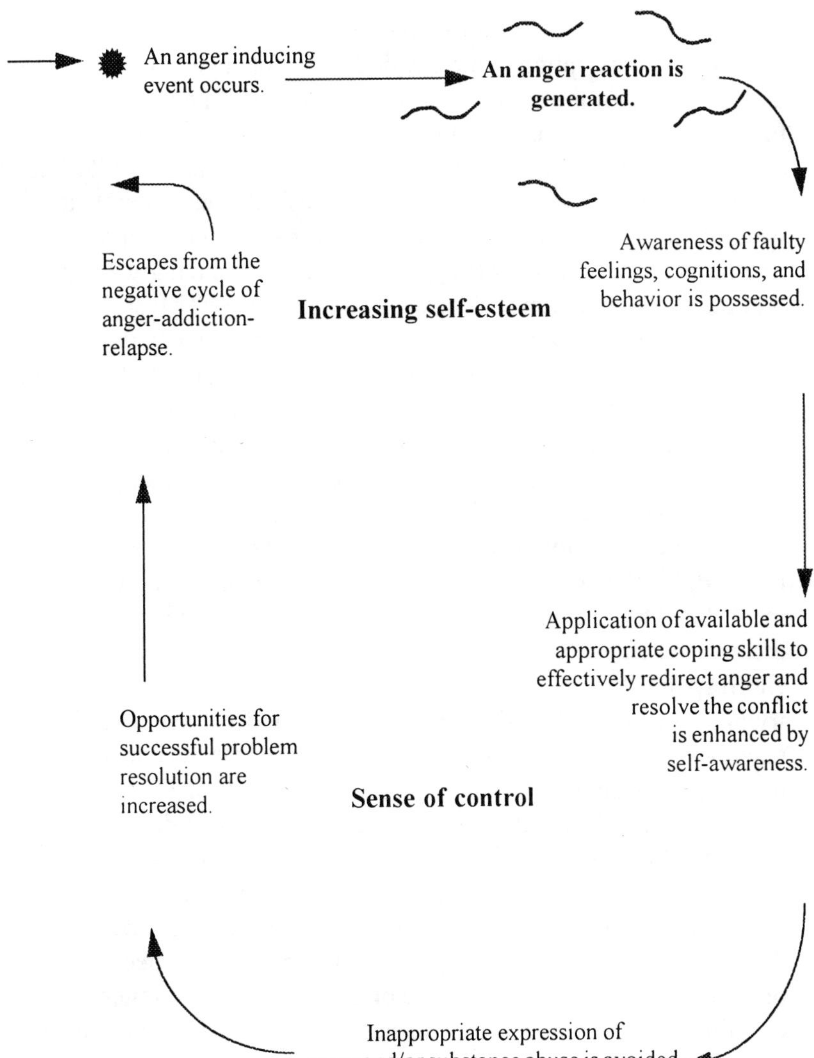

*The individual identifies strategies to modify self-destructive feelings, thoughts, and behaviors and selects response choices that allows him or her to escape the anger-addiction-relapse cycle. This success reinforces the belief that change *is* possible.

constructively redirect response choices (Chapters 5–13). Teaching clients to capitalize on control points in the reaction-response cycle dramatically reduces their relapse potential.

A brief description of the physical basis for anger enhances clients' understanding of the anger reaction. The concept of anger being a mixture of pain and fear is introduced to identify the instinctual, predetermined component of anger (Fonberg, 1979; MacLean, 1955; Moyer, 1976; Schachter, 1957, 1971). Clients are asked to envision themselves walking through the woods. They come over a rise and see a wolf caught in a hunter's trap. The wolf appears to be experiencing great pain, so they attempt to intervene. What is the wolf's reaction? Most clients state, "It will try to chew your arm off!" When asked to clarify the wolf's reaction, they explain that the wolf was in pain and afraid of having further pain inflicted, so it instinctively defended itself. An analogy to human behavior is then drawn. Imagine a man swimming in a lake. Suddenly, he develops a leg cramp and experiences difficulty staying afloat. You are on the shore and see this event unfolding. You quickly dive in and swim to the individual's rescue. What is his reaction? Most clients will respond, "The person might start grabbing me and struggling against me. When I try to calm him down, he fights harder and ignores my comments." When asked to explain this seemingly irrational behavior, clients respond, "The person was scared and in pain; he fought instinctively trying to survive." The similarity between the wolf's and the human's reactions are identified, so that clients can appreciate the impact of predatory and defensive reactions.

To further illustrate the unconscious dynamics driving these reactions, a brief review of the physiology of the brain is given. Leeper (1968), MacLean (1955), Moyer (1976), and Schachter (1957) provide an excellent description of this process. The limbic system is identified as the seat of all emotions, generating split-second decisions based on incoming stimuli that alert the brain of imminent danger, pleasure, or pain. The amygdala, a tiny structure located inside the limbic system, is identified and likened to a telephone answering machine, with the critical difference being that an answering machine allows the individual a choice in which calls are accepted, whereas the amygdala processes *all* calls—regardless of your wishes! This involuntary process is the initial step in the reactive phase of anger. Clients are instructed that these instinctual reactions are *not* amenable to change, but that faulty misperceptions that stimulate aggressive responses can be identified and modified.

The role of the hypothalamus (Moyer, 1976) is also identified, since this structure is the seat of all aggressive reactions. A comparison of three basic aggressive reactions is provided, so that clients understand which components of the anger reaction can and cannot be impacted by anger management-relapse prevention training. The first type of aggressive reaction is defined as a primitive, instinctual reaction based on fear or pain (remember our earlier examples of the wolf and the drowning man)—*the fight or flight syndrome* (Schachter, 1957). Mobilization of this aggressive reaction activates the central nervous system to prepare the body for a fight or for flight. If the perceived threat is not quickly eliminated, the adrenal glands are activated and secrete epinephrine and norepinephrine to strengthen and sustain the central nervous system response. This "gut-level" reaction does *not* involve conscious thought. The sole purpose of this reaction is to preserve the physical integrity of the organism. This type of aggression, as discussed earlier, is *not* amenable to change; however, misinterpretations of incoming stimuli can be consciously challenged (see Chapter 6).

The second type of aggressive reaction is called *defensive aggression* and also serves the purpose of self-preservation. Unlike predatory aggression, this reaction involves higher level thought processes. The individual can rapidly assess options *before* selecting a response. An example I frequently use is a potential rape. I begin by saying that I am leaving a shopping mall alone at night. I see a group of men across the parking lot and they look my way. I have my car key ready and I acknowledge their presence with a hello. I continue to move toward my car, and they begin to follow me. I start running, yelling "Fire! fire!" They chase me into an isolated corner of the parking lot, so I begin by saying, "My name is Jo, I have three children, I'm a social worker, I am a person!" This fails, so I proceed to explain that I have AIDS or herpes and am not a safe sexual partner. They continue their advances, so I defecate and urinate in my pants and attempt to vomit. If this is unsuccessful, I resort to physical defense through aggressive behavior. This all might happen in a 2- to 3-minute time span, but the example clearly illustrates the involvement of thought in this defensive aggressive reaction. It becomes problematic when incoming stimuli are misinterpreted and threat is experienced without the presence of true danger.

Defensive aggression is healthy, and need not be addressed unless repeated misinterpretation of incoming stimuli generates a pattern of inappropriate responses (aggressive verbal or physical behavior without just cause).

The final type of aggressive reaction is identified as *irritable aggression*. This reaction is generated by some noxious, but not life-threatening, event that interferes with some aspect of daily functioning. Examples include a nagging significant other, traffic jams, a flat tire, a disagreement with your boss, a deadline that is unreasonable, not getting accepted for a job, ripping your pants while out in public. This list goes on and on. Irritable aggression is a primary focus of the anger management-relapse prevention training program since it affects feelings, cognitions, and behaviors, and significantly influences relapse potential (Daley, 1988; Ellis et al., 1988; Gorski & Miller, 1986; Potter-Efron, 1990).

A brief review of the physiology of addiction follows the discussion on anger reactions. Again, the goal is to help clients assess factors they can and cannot alter so that during later stages of treatment they can be held accountable for response choices related to sobriety and anger management. A review of the disease concept of addiction is presented (Gorski & Miller, 1986; Leiber et al., 1975; Mello, 1972; Milam & Ketcham, 1981; Nathan et al., 1970; Schuckit et al., 1985; Vaillant, 1983) followed by a discussion of the post-acute withdrawal syndrome outlined in Gorski and Miller (1986). Post-acute withdrawal is identified as emotional overreaction and stress sensitivity secondary to central nervous system damage acquired while actively drinking or abusing drugs. Gorski and Miller (1986) state that this syndrome can occur 3 to 6 months after abstinence is achieved, since central nervous system adjustments can take from 6 to 24 months. This biological hypersensitivity, when combined with an aggressive reaction, can significantly influence relapse potential unless active steps are taken to dilute these variables.

Once the physiology of anger and addiction are explained, the focus turns to psychosocial factors influencing the anger-relapse cycle. Key elements include patterns of learned behavior (Bandura, 1969, 1971a, 1971b, 1974, 1977, 1986; Barlow, 1978; Bellack & Hersen, 1985; Patterson, 1985; Thoresen & Coates, 1980), accuracy of interpretations, and effectiveness of existing responses. When reviewing patterns of learned behavior, clients are invited to explore past role models and the feelings, thoughts, and behaviors overtly and covertly demonstrated in these primary relationships. The goal is to identify patterns of response, both for the expression of anger and for substance use, as preparation for learning and applying rational-emotive and cognitive-behavioral techniques. This element is the topic of Chapter 3.

A second element involves accuracy of our interpretations and the interplay between past experiences, their outcomes, and our present emotional state. If we have painful memories of an experience similar to a current situation, and our emotional state is unstable, we are vulnerable to cognitive distortions and faulty response choices. Conversely, if past experiences have been pleasurable and our emotional state is stable, response choices will be more appropriate. Although proponents of rational-emotive and cognitive-behavioral approaches diminish the importance of past experiences, I see them as critically linked to individuals' current response choices. A recent example occurred in my anger management-relapse prevention training program. To illustrate the role of past experiences in shaping current interpretations, I asked the group to define the term "social worker." Responses included the following: somebody who gives out bus tokens; a person who does housing referrals; a worthless S.O.B.; somebody who takes kids away from their families; a helper; a therapist like you Jo. . . . I then asked the group to identify their past experiences with social workers. The current responses were directly linked to experiences from the past that were perceived as positive or negative.

A second example involves a group of veterans with posttraumatic stress disorder. In one of my sessions I used the term "neutralize" to describe a process of diminishing negative responses. The reaction of group members ranged from silence to open displays of agitation. Since I know my group members well and am liked by them, I pursued the reaction to identify its source. These clients are combat veterans who served in Vietnam, so the word "neutralize" was seen as an extremely offensive term, since in Vietnam it meant quite literally to destroy anything and everything in one's path. This example again illustrates the linkage between past experiences, current interpretations, and response choices. I believe clients *must* grasp this critical connection before patterns of self-defeating feelings, cognitions, and behavior can be arrested.

The final element involves the effectiveness of existing responses. When we fail to receive negative consequences for inappropriate response choices, motivation for change is minimal. If I can scream and yell and get my way, or brood and keep the whole family on eggshells, why would I want to change? If I can drink and/or use drugs, spend all my money on pursuing my addiction, and avoid responsibility for the consequences of my actions, what would motivate me to change? If, on the other hand, my response choices generate a pattern of relationship losses, employment terminations, legal charges, health consequences, or a spiritual crisis, I might become more receptive to change. Helping clients link actions to consequences, in regard to both anger and the relapse process, is essential if quality sobriety is the desired result.

The final objective of Session 1 is to identify the relationship between anger and addiction that perpetuates the relapse cycle. In developing my models, I reviewed the work of several well-known professionals. Gorski and Miller (1986) identify seven stages in their developmental model of recovery: pretreatment, a motivational crisis, stabilization, early recovery, middle recovery, late recovery, and maintenance. Since recovery is a continuous process of evolution, these stages are not completed in a linear fashion. Clients are at risk for setbacks, identified as "stuck points," at any time during the recovery process; however, they are particularly vulnerable when in transition between stages. Failure to address these "stuck points" can lead to regression, identified as "partial recovery" or relapse. Gorski and Miller (1986) identify a multifaceted model of relapse that contains a number of self-defeating thoughts, feelings, and behavior. To arrest the relapse process, clients must maintain abstinence and initiate a series of daily tasks to manage symptoms of post-acute withdrawal and promote the correction of biopsychosocial damage caused by addiction.

Potter-Efron and Potter-Efron (1991a) identify models of normal anger and chronic anger. Normal anger is defined as a process of beginning awareness, excitement, action, contact, and withdrawal. This is viewed as a healthy process through which anger is constructively redirected to reduce conflict. Chronic anger involves oversensitivity to anger cues during the beginning awareness stage, which leads to intense focus on anger, impulsive responses, an anger high, and the inability to withdraw from conflict. This model of anger is seen as highly destructive to recovery and is often viewed as a defense against shame (Potter-Efron, 1989, 1990; Potter-Efron, P., & Potter-Efron, 1991; Potter-Efron & Potter-Efron, 1989, 1991a, 1991b).

Ellis et al. (1988) postulate that irrational beliefs lead to low frustration tolerance. The resulting discomfort creates anticipatory responses of a pain/fear-based nature, which foster impulsive, self-destructive thoughts and behavior. If the individual lacks adequate coping skills to interrupt this process, the cycle is maintained or escalates to a higher level of dysfunctional response.

Finally, DiClemente (1993) identifies a transtheoretical model comprised of five distinct stages: precontemplation, preparation, action, maintenance, and relapse/recycle. This model promotes the belief that recovery is a process of awareness, evaluation, intervention, reinforcement, and reevaluation/modification. Clients can repeat these processes multiple times, and their progress is enhanced by designing an appropriate "fit" between interventions and the client's stage of change. DiClemente (1993) further identifies the role of self-efficacy in client outcomes. Clients who perceive themselves as capable of initiating long-term success achieved greater success than did those with lower self-efficacy ratings.

I borrow elements from each of the preceding approaches. Key factors in the anger management-relapse prevention models involve the interplay between cognitions and availability/absence of appropriate coping skills to redirect anger and reduce relapse potential. When clients lack awareness of their current feelings, thoughts, and behaviors and of the role these factors have in the relapse process and, further, do not possess adequate coping skills to redirect anger, the potential for returning to former patterns of self-defeating response choices is high. Conversely, once clients learn to recognize faulty patterns of feeling, thinking, and behaving, and develop adequate coping skills, their relapse potential is significantly reduced (see Figures 1 and 2).

3

The Impact of Past Experiences on Current Feelings, Thoughts, and Response Choices

Session 2 involves an exploration of past experiences and their impact on current response choices. Although I uphold many beliefs espoused by rational-emotive and cognitive-behavioral approaches, there are significant differences in this program regarding use of the past to aid clients in their search for self-acceptance, understanding, and lasting behavior change. Rational-emotive therapy acknowledges that biological, cultural, and environmental factors influence human functioning, emphasizing that irrational beliefs, learned from significant others in childhood, generate a process of autosuggestion and self-repetition that perpetuates irrational beliefs in the here and now (Ellis, 1962, 1971, 1973, 1985, 1987a; Ellis & Becker, 1982; Ellis & Bernard, 1984, 1985; Ellis & Grieger, 1977, 1986; Ellis & Harper, 1975). According to Ellis (1988), since we create our own disturbed feelings and thoughts, we have the power to reframe them.

I agree with this basic tenet of rational-emotive therapy. However, my viewpoint diverges in regard to the client's need for acceptance and love. Rational-emotive therapy purports that individuals do not *need* to be loved and accepted, though it may be desirable (Ellis, 1988). This appears contradictory to the belief that blame is the core of most emotional disturbances (Ellis, 1987a), especially when working with addicted populations. If clients cannot achieve love and acceptance from self and others, how then are they to overcome the shame and blame so characteristic of addictive disease? Revisiting the past is used in the anger management-relapse prevention training program to help clients understand their response choices, make adjustments when needed, and remember but let go of painful past experiences that influence current feelings, thoughts, and behavior. These steps are critical to the release of shame and blame, which is necessary to interrupt the anger-relapse cycle. Much like a lock combination, all the tumblers must line up for the safe to open. In this case, a combination of awareness, availability of coping skills, and client motivation to initiate change must fall into place before quality recovery becomes a possibility.

Beck's (1987) cognitive therapy places little emphasis on the role past experiences play in current thoughts and behavior. This approach is based on the belief that feelings and behavior are determined by how individuals interpret life experiences. The central concept of Beck's model is that emotional disturbance can best be understood by focusing on the cognitive content of an individual's reactions to upsetting thoughts and/or events (DeRubeis & Beck, 1988). I believe that a structured review of past events and their symbolic meaning to clients on an affective level must occur before awareness of cognitions is possible. Emotions generate cognitions, which in turn influence behaviors. This is especially critical when working with chemically dependent clients. The unwritten rule "don't feel" promotes distortions in thoughts and behavior. Guiding clients through a painful but healing exploration of past events prepares them for the recovery-oriented activities outlined in Chapters 5–13.

Meichenbaum (1977, 1986) provides yet another view of emotional disturbance and acknowledges that past experiences influence cognitions. He believes that self-statements affect behavior as significantly as do statements made by others. According to this premise, the prerequisite for behavior change is two-fold: (1) client awareness of feelings, thoughts, behaviors, and the impact these factors have on others, and (2) client interruption of the scripted nature of his or her behavior so responses can be evaluated situationally (Meichenbaum, 1986). I support the belief that emotional disturbances are the combined result of thoughts, feelings, and behaviors. Revisiting the past, framed as an educational component of the recovery process, allows clients to identify patterns of feeling, thinking, and behaving that shape present response choices. The goal is *not* to blame self or others, focus on losses, or participate in "if only I had/had not . . ." exercises in futility. Rather, it is designed to foster insight regarding determinants of individual personality styles. This process empowers clients to reformulate current feelings, thoughts, and response choices. It also erodes the rationalization "my past determines my future," challenging clients to assume responsibility for current and future feelings, thoughts, and behavior. Although we cannot change where we have been, we *can* influence where we are going.

Finally, Patterson (1985), who conducted a microsocial analysis of angry and irritable behavior, holds the conviction that families "train" each other to be violent. He identifies the goal of therapy as increased client awareness of family patterns to break family-of-origin connections that anchor current response styles. I also believe that family dynamics shape feelings, thoughts, and behaviors, but I feel most information is transmitted without conscious awareness and without malicious intent. Mr. X., a client with impulse control disorder and substance dependency, is a good example of the insidious nature of this process.

Mr. X. is a middle-aged man with a history of violence and substance abuse dating back to early childhood. When he began the anger management-relapse prevention training program he was unable to identify the origin of his response choices with respect to anger or substance abuse. An exploration of past experiences, especially during early developmental stages, revealed a family pattern of violence and substance abuse. This behavior was viewed as expected and normal for members of this family, and deviation was viewed as disloyalty. This pattern was innocuously passed from generation to generation and became so ingrained that my client failed to identify the connection between past experiences, current feelings, thoughts, and behavior, and the negative consequences he encountered throughout his life. After participating in Session 2 (outlined later in this chapter), and maintaining an anger management-relapse prevention journal (described in Chapter 4), he began to identify linkages between these factors. He realized that now that he understood the basis for why he felt, thought, and behaved as he did, he had greater control in making choices to perpetuate this cycle or to generate healthier lifestyle choices. Framing family patterns as unconscious processes perpetuated by lack of insight rather than by deliberate acts of destruction reduces resentment and allows clients to view others, even parents, as fallible and imperfect.

To highlight the importance of client insight and motivation in eliciting cognitive and behavioral change, Sessions 2–4 of the anger management-relapse prevention training program incorporate the first three stages of DiClemente's (1993) transtheoretical model of change. Stage 1, called precontemplation, postulates that clients lack awareness of existing problems or, if problems are acknowledged, see no need to initiate change. A classic example is an alcoholic who admits to having an occasional drink "to socialize" and sees no reason to give up alcohol completely. Stage 2, contemplation, is a stage of evaluation wherein the client seriously considers the problem and possibility of change. This involves reviewing current response choices and their consequences. For example, a third DWI arrest might prompt contemplation as the individual evaluates the relative benefits and costs of driving under the influence. The third stage, preparation, involves commitment to change, laying the groundwork to initiate it. During this stage the alcoholic identifies his or her alcohol problem and takes initial steps to curb the addiction. DiClemente's final three stages—action, maintenance, and relapse and recycle—are the focus of Stages 2 and 3 of my model: Sessions 5–12 and the anger-process aftercare group. The remainder of this chapter will address Session 2, the impact of past experiences on current feelings, thoughts, and behavior.

Session 2 is often the most painful exercise through which clients must pass before reaching a point of readiness for change. When opening this session, it is critical to remind clients the purpose of this exercise is *not* to punish themselves or others for past behaviors, since people generally do the best they can with their available skills. The absurdity of the cliché "If I knew then what I know now life would be very different" is emphasized, since we cannot turn back time. We *can*, however, learn from past experiences and develop strategies to alter the course of current life choices. Clients are encouraged to view this exercise as a window through which past experiences, and their impact on current feelings, thoughts, and response choices, can be identified and disarmed.

Following this introduction, clients are invited to consider two critical elements of the self: the child within, the little boy or girl who experienced the situations under review, and the man or woman that the boy or girl became as life experiences unfolded. This focus on the evolution of self helps clients recapture feelings and thoughts buried behind walls of denial, fear, pain, and shame. The goal is to generate an emotional catharsis powerful enough to begin the process of breaking down defenses that fuel the anger-relapse cycle.

Once this foundation is established, clients are given a written exercise structured to provide a safe, yet painful, exploration of their past (see Worksheet 1, pp. 162–163). They are encouraged to be as accurate as possible when completing the exercise, and assured that information revealed remains within their personal control. This emphasis on client-directed participation breaks down resistance and fosters communication and trust between group members and the leader—factors critical to successful participation in the therapeutic process.

Several tasks must be accomplished during this session for clients to successfully transform self-defeating patterns of feeling, thinking, and behaving into heightened awareness and personal growth. First, clients must identify the association between messages they received from primary role models during childhood and the power these messages had, and continue to exert, in defining clients' frame of reference for viewing life experiences. Second, clients must address and overcome residual confusion, created by contradictory messages from the past, so they can escape the cycle of self-defeating life choices preventing the attainment of quality sobriety.

Group members are given a brief explanation of the worksheet and allowed 10–15 minutes to complete the exercise. Volunteers are then "recruited" to share their responses, with the intention of using peer modeling to encourage all members to share responses by the session's end. This review process frequently uncovers painful memories and evokes powerful emotional reactions in clients. The primary tasks of the group leader are to assist clients in staying focused on the cleansing aspects of the review and to provide a safe, nonjudgmental environment to begin the process of resolution.

When resistance is encountered, as it inevitably will be, clients are invited to explore the origin of the resistance: Do they feel afraid, vulnerable, sad, abandoned, angry? What is their fantasy about what will happen if they reveal their responses to the group? They are also encouraged to consider how damaging this material has been, and will continue to be, until they identify, process, and resolve it. Since themes (past abuse, neglect, abandonment, family chaos) generally arise as members share their responses, even the most resistant clients begin to see they are not alone. Framed as a "readiness issue," with individual members having variable degrees of readiness to explore past experiences, members are not penalized if they elect not to participate. Since I always go with resistance, rarely will a client reach the end of the session refusing to participate on any level. Once this process is complete, clients are ready to move on to Session 3: identifying triggers and cues.

4

Recognition of Triggers and Cues

A frequent justification offered to explain relapse is "It caught me off guard—I had *no idea* I was building up to drink!" A similar response is common from clients who misdirect anger, then indignantly retort, "If I had *known* I was about to act that way, don't you think I would have *done* something about it?" In both cases clients fail to recognize subtle changes in physiology (breathing, heart rate, muscle tone), feelings (fear, anger, confusion), thoughts (the internal dialogue activated by incoming stimuli), and behavior (visible shifts in posture, gestures, verbalizations, facial expressions) that precede the selection of response choices (Annis, 1986; Annis & Davis, 1987a, 1987b; Daley, 1988; Gorski & Miller, 1986; Marlatt & George, 1984; Marlatt & Gordon, 1985; Mueller & Ketcham, 1987; Potter-Efron & Potter-Efron, 1991a). Their inability to recognize that relapse, be it the inappropriate expression of anger, substance abuse, or both, is a *process* that creates a sense of helplessness that perpetuates the anger-relapse cycle.

Walker (1980), in describing the battered woman syndrome, identifies three stages in the anger-aggression-explosion cycle. First, a gradual buildup of emotions and aggressive thoughts occurs. This process escalates and culminates in a battering episode. Following the explosion, a period of remorse and/or relief occurs, during which the abusive partner is loving and generous to his victim. After a brief "honeymoon" period, the buildup stage begins again. A similar dynamic activates the relapse cycle. During the buildup stage, changes occur in feelings, thoughts, and behavior. The addict/alcoholic begins to feel angry, frustrated, or deprived. This is followed by rationalizations justifying why he or she should be allowed to use drugs or drink: "Everybody else does; surely one time won't make any difference." "I've been sober for 6 months, and it's my birthday, I deserve to relax!" "I'm tired of being a goodie two shoes; it hasn't changed anything anyway!" These thoughts, referred to as "stinking thinking" (Anonymous, 1976), generate high-risk behaviors: calling up old buddies who still drink or use drugs, frequenting former hangouts, withdrawing from support networks, or ignoring feedback from significant others. This process culminates in a relapse episode, followed by a period of guilt, shame, anger, self-blame, and promises that it will never happen again. If this cycle is not interrupted, the individual will experience a brief "honeymoon" period followed by reactivation of the buildup stage, starting the process over again (Annis, 1986; Annis & Davis, 1987a, 1987b; Daley, 1988; Gorski & Miller, 1986; Marlatt & George, 1984; Marlatt & Gordon, 1985; Mueller & Ketcham, 1987; Potter-Efron & Potter-Efron, 1991a).

Session 3 is designed to help clients make the critical connection between the buildup phase and their subsequent response choices. Clients are taught to recognize physical, emotional, cognitive, and behavioral cues that fuel the anger relapse cycle unless identified and disarmed. Emphasis is placed on the potential use of these warning signs as frontline defenses for arresting the relapse process. Since efficacy expectations (one's belief about whether one possesses the ability to execute certain actions) and outcome expectations (one's belief regarding one's potential to modify consequences) significantly influence treatment outcomes, teaching clients to identify cues and the tactics necessary to disarm them is paramount to the intervention process (Annis, 1986; Annis & Davis, 1987a, 1987b; Daley, 1988; Gorski & Miller, 1986; Marlatt & George, 1984; Marlatt & Gordon, 1985; Mueller & Ketcham, 1987; Potter-Efron & Potter-Efron, 1991a).

When teaching clients to recognize the buildup stage, a useful analogy is the behavior of a rattlesnake. A rattlesnake rarely strikes without warning. I have never seen a rattlesnake jump up, race across a field, and attack without provocation. There are usually a series of reactions prior to the strike: First, the snake will hiss and coil up. If the threatening object continues to approach, the snake begins to rattle its tail. The closer the object approaches, the more vigorous is the rattle. A final warning occurs when the snake assumes an attack stance. If the object continues its approach, the snake, as a last resort, strikes. Human beings, much like rattlesnakes, rarely strike without warning. Again, there are a series of reactions (shifts in feelings and thoughts) that occur prior to a behavioral response. Recognizing this process of escalation is the first step in relapse prevention.

During this session clients participate in an exercise designed to identify their physical, emotional, cognitive, and behavioral reactions to their environment. A worksheet, adapted from Sonkin & Durphy (1985), provides the framework for this activity (see Worksheet 2, pp. 164–167). Clients are encouraged to identify cues from each of the above categories and rank order them according to the sequence of their appearance. An example will help illustrate this process. I am sitting in my doctor's office at 2:45 P.M. in anticipation of a 3:00 P.M. appointment. At 3:20, I begin to feel agitated that I have not been called by the nurse. As time goes on, I start thinking about how inefficient this doctor's office is. By 3:30 I tell myself that if I ran my business this way, I would be fired. At 3:45 I begin to rattle my magazine, clear my throat, and wiggle in my chair, hoping to draw attention to the fact I have been waiting long beyond my appointment time. By 4:00 I am so angry I either leave without being seen or approach the receptionist, rudely demanding to be seen immediately "or heads will roll."

Had I been aware of my initial agitation, I could have initiated an intervention to interrupt this process. At 3:15, I might have approached the receptionist to inquire how long the wait might be. This would have defused my agitation, since the receptionist's response, "Only a few more minutes, thanks for your patience," or "I'm sorry, the doctor had an emergency and is running about an hour and a half behind schedule" would have provided me with the opportunity to make choices about how best to handle the situation (deciding to wait or rescheduling for another time).

The preceding example illustrates the importance of cue recognition as a critical step in determining response choices. If I am unaware of the gradual escalation of my anger as this event unfolds (the buildup of emotional agitation, angry thoughts, agitated behavior, and finally a hostile response), I will initiate a hostile response without realizing I had alternative choices at various points along the way. Learning to recognize cues, and the order of their appearance, allows us to initiate interventions *before* the buildup becomes so pronounced that we withdraw, explode, or, in the case of addiction, relapse.

Since individuals do not routinely evaluate their physical reactions, feelings, thoughts, behaviors, and the triggers that elicit and ultimately define response choices, an explanation of each category is provided before clients complete the triggers and cues awareness worksheet. Beginning with physical reactions, clients are instructed to think of changes they experience *within their bodies* when angered or craving substances. Examples include an elevated heart rate, increased respiration, muscle tension in various parts of the body, and other physiological changes *not readily observable* by others. Clients are asked to identify these changes according to the order of their appearance. Again, the goal of rank ordering reactions is to develop early awareness of warning signs *before* it is too late to implement appropriate response choices. If I am aware that first my heart begins pounding, then I experience neck tension followed by tightness in my stomach and finally a sensation of being lightheaded before I start cursing and swinging, I have several opportunities to interrupt this process before my aggressive response occurs. By the time I feel lightheaded, it may be too late; however, if I intervene at any point preceding this reaction, I still have time to abort my aggressive response.

The second category involves emotional reactions. Clients are asked to identify their *feelings* (anger, sadness, fear, happiness, confusion) as specific events unfold. This process is especially difficult for clients recovering from substance abuse disorders, since "don't feel" is a central rule in dysfunctional family systems. Clients are reassured that if they are unable to identify feelings, the leader and fellow group members will help them when worksheets are shared later in the session.

The third category involves cognitions. Clients are asked to identify thoughts they experience as specific events unfold. The following questions are helpful in stimulating answers for this category: "Are your thoughts neutral, happy, fearful, sad, angry, or confused?" (Again, this is difficult for clients in recovery from substance abuse disorders.) "If you were a court reporter recording your thoughts word for word, what *exactly* are you saying to yourself?" "Are your thoughts designed to excuse behaviors or blame others for your current situation?" These sample questions help clients focus on both the process and content of internal dialogues that influence response choices.

The fourth category involves behavioral cues, defined as what you do, *not* how you feel inside. These are observable signs that others can readily recognize. Clients are instructed to identify changes in their behavior that occur as anger escalates or the desire to use substances becomes more urgent. Examples include pacing or aimless wandering, fist clenching and unclenching, withdrawal and pouting, gesturing (including obscene motions with any part of the body), frequenting high-risk settings, or avoiding support group meetings. As with each of the preceding categories, clients are asked to rank reactions according to their appearance. The goal is to identify subtle shifts in behavior before more overt, potentially negative, behaviors come to pass.

A final component of this exercise involves examining specific environmental factors that generate irritable reactions and increase relapse potential. These include, but are not limited to, people (family members, friends, coworkers, strangers), places (bars, stores, banks, freeways), specific times (times of the day, week, year, or holidays), and events (frustrating situations that individuals encounter during the course of daily life). Although some factors can be neutralized, many are beyond our control. Clients frequently complain, "What's the use of knowing what bugs me if I can't change it?" Remind them that awareness affords the advantage of choice, so when high-risk factors *do* arise, they will be prepared to respond accordingly. We may lack the power necessary to change circumstances, but each of us has the potential to direct our personal response choices!

In processing this exercise, group members are asked to share one category at a time, and a list of physical reactions, feelings, cognitions, behaviors, and environmental factors triggering these cues is constructed on the board. Next, categories are combined, so clients can develop a hierarchy of cues and identify triggers contributing to this process. Once developed, this hierarchy, much like a security alarm, provides advance warning that potentially negative response choices (stuffing or exploding anger, or relapse) are imminent. When this warning is heeded, coping strategies can be applied to prevent negative consequences. The goal is to identify similarities and differences in both cues and triggers so that clients can appreciate the unique nature of this process. What one person finds offensive, another may disregard, leading to dramatic differences in the stimulation of cues and subsequent response choices. A recent example from this session of my training program will better illustrate this concept.

I routinely set up scenarios to elicit client reactions. In this instance, I indicated that I was born and raised in Pasadena, Texas, and asked clients to identify their impressions of this geographic location. One client said the words "Pasadena, Texas" made him feel warm and happy, since he equated this location with horses, country western music, and Tex-Mex food—all things he greatly enjoyed. As this client shared his impressions, I observed a very strong negative reaction in one of my black clients. When asked to identify the source of his distress, he indicated that Pasadena has another connotation to him—the Ku Klux Klan. He explained his family had been subjected to prejudice that severely influenced his early childhood. The same words that elicited pleasant cues from the first client created anger and distrust in another. This example concluded with clients agreeing that who, what, when, where, and how are all variables that impact their cues, triggers, and response choices. The majority agreed that awareness of these factors greatly enhances their potential to modify unproductive response choices.

Highly resistant clients may continue to challenge the usefulness of this exercise, or may inform you that they have no idea what environmental factors affect them, much less what their physical, emotional, cognitive, and behavioral reactions are. This creates an opening to introduce the anger management-relapse prevention journal. Adapted from the work of Sonkin and Durphy (1985) and Daley (1988), this journal is designed to help clients track physical reactions, emotions, thoughts, and behaviors across time, so that patterns can be identified and response choices modified, if warranted (see Worksheet 3, pp. 168–171). Clients are instructed to make entries as often as necessary and to include any incidents linked to anger or urges to abuse substances. Anger is defined as a continuum from mild irritation to rage, with many points along the scale. Clients are encouraged to count mild irritations, since the cumulative effect of multiple small frustrations, not effectively disarmed, can be significant. Urges to use substances are defined similarly, and clients are again cautioned to attend to small cues since the cumulative effect can generate a relapse episode.

The most significant downfall of the journal is client reluctance to use it on a consistent basis. When clients tell me, "Mrs. Clancy, I'm too busy to write in the journal," I use the following approach:

Therapist: "Do you brush your teeth before bed?"

Client: "Yes."

Therapist: "Do you use the bathroom before bed too?"

Client: "Everybody does, why?"

Therapist: "How long does it take you to do these tasks?"

Client: "About five minutes."

Therapist: "Well, the journal is designed with easy-to-use preprinted forms that only take a few minutes to complete. If you add it to your bedtime routine, it will be a snap!"

This approach has some success with *motivated* clients. Those who continue to resist are reminded that the journal is for their benefit, not mine, and that they will only get out of training what they are willing to put into it.

Completion of Session 3 marks the end of Phase 1 in the anger management-relapse prevention training program. Phase 1, much like the blueprints for a house, provides a schematic so clients can recognize and understand personal response choices and the factors that shaped and continue to influence life experiences. Phase 1 also creates a foundation upon which interventions necessary for modification of unproductive response choices can be built. Sessions 4–12 introduce action strategies for change. These strategies, similar to the action stage of DiClemente's (1993) transtheoretical model of change, can be used separately or in combination and can be learned and applied in any order. Chapter 5 introduces the time-out technique, the first of nine strategies presented in this book.

Part 2

Action Strategies for Change

FOCUS: The acquisition of coping skills designed to reduce inappropriate expressions of anger and relapse

5

The Time-Out Technique

Part 2 of this book marks the beginning of skills acquisition. Clients participate in 9 weeks of intensive training that exposes them to a variety of options for the redirection of anger and relapse urges. Each session introduces a new skill presented by using a combination of didactic instruction, group discussion, worksheets, group exercises, and role plays. Chapters 5–13 provide in-depth discussion of each specific technique. Worksheets and group exercises necessary to replicate each session are included, and, when appropriate, case studies are provided to illustrate skills application. This chapter is dedicated to a discussion of the time-out technique, which is presented to clients in Session 4.

The time-out technique, an aversive behavior therapy intervention, is based on the principles of operant conditioning as described by Skinner (1948, 1971). Skinner's model maintains that learning cannot occur in the absence of reinforcement. Behaviors that are rewarded (positive reinforcement) tend to be repeated, and those that are discouraged (negative reinforcement) are eliminated. When defining the reinforcing qualities of the time-out technique, Barlow (1978) describes this approach as time-out from positive reinforcement. His assumption is that target behaviors will decrease in frequency if opportunities for positive reinforcement are denied. An example is the removal of a misbehaving child from the family room to an isolated corner in another room. The removal from positive reinforcement, an opportunity to interact with other family members, in theory will diminish negative behaviors linked to initiation of the time-out procedure.

The use of Antabuse with chronically relapsing alcoholics has a similar effect, based on the principles of negative reinforcement (Mueller & Ketcham, 1987). An alcoholic participating in Antabuse therapy will become violently ill if alcohol is ingested. Since this medication blocks the metabolism of alcohol by the liver, drinking generates toxic results. The desire to avoid unpleasant physical reactions that result from mixing Antabuse and alcohol negatively reinforces the avoidance of alcoholic beverages.

I define time-out somewhat differently. My contention is that time-out is an opportunity to step back and consider options before committing oneself to a particular course of action. Functioning under the principle of negative reinforcement, the goal is to avoid response choices that activate the anger-relapse cycle. Potter-Efron and Potter-Efron (1991a) and Sonkin and Durphy (1985) identify the need to recognize when anger is escalating in order to allow opportunities for application of the time-out technique and avoidance of explosive behavior. Daley (1988) provides similar instructions for identifying and heeding warning signs to promote relapse prevention. I expand the use of this technique to encompass the redirection of implosive as well as explosive anger when working toward relapse prevention. An analogy describing the demolition of a building elucidates this notion. When a demolition crew is contracted to bring down a building, they have two options: Explosive charges can be placed to either explode or implode the building. If the building is located in a populated area, implosion is selected to avoid scattering debris and causing possible injury to bystanders. If, however, the building is isolated, the demolition crew may elect to explode it, since there is no risk of damage to other structures or people. Whether the building is imploded and caves in on itself, or exploded and scattered in all directions, the end result is the same: The building is destroyed. When applied to the concept of relapse prevention, anger, whether imploded ("stuffed") or exploded, creates a tremendous potential for relapse. Application of the time-out technique, and modified versions of this intervention, can greatly reduce the potential for negative outcomes.

As previously stated, time-out is especially useful when working with addicts and alcoholics since chronic anger is a primary issue in the recovery process (Hecker & Lunde, 1985; Potter-Efron, P. & Potter-Efron, 1991; Spielberger, 1988; Spielberger, Krasner, & Solomon, 1988; Walfish, 1990). Deschner (1984) provides an overview of the traditional time-out technique, creating a foundation upon which modifications to reduce risk factors of relapse can be built. These variations provide avenues for relapse prevention when the traditional approach cannot be successfully applied. A description of the traditional technique is helpful before identifying alternatives.

The traditional time-out technique involves the following steps:

1. Decide when you are beginning to get angry.
2. Identify your need to take a time-out.
3. Leave quietly and engage in an activity to reduce your anger.
4. Return and exchange "technical errors" with your partner so resolution of the conflict can be achieved.

To avoid misuse of this technique, a clarification of time-out versus avoidance is necessary. Time-out, as I define it, serves the purpose of providing opportunities to consider options before committing oneself to action. Effective use of this technique involves removing oneself from the situation triggering anger or relapse urges, carefully considering available options, and returning to the situation for problem resolution. Failure to complete this process (i.e., leaving and then holding onto anger and refusing to return and resolve the conflict) can increase relapse potential. Potter-Efron and Potter-Efron (Potter-Efron, P. & Potter-Efron, 1991; Potter-Efron & Potter-Efron, 1991a, 1991b) identify the *quality* of time-out as critical in determination of outcome expectancies. The importance of applying positive self-talk (the topic of Chapter 6) during time-out to defuse anger and relapse urges, followed by a return to the situation for resolution of the problem, if possible, is emphasized.

There are, of course, exceptions that prohibit return and resolution. However, processing the event is still necessary to defuse anger and relapse potential. If the situation involves intoxicated, psychotic, or rageful individuals who are strangers you will never see again, return and resolution are often impossible. The goal in such situations is to remove oneself to a neutral setting to avoid response choices with potentially negative consequences (physical confrontation, implosive anger ending in relapse). Although the traditional technique must be modified, it remains imperative to apply positive self-talk ("Gee, that person was really out of control; I need to avoid taking that situation personally since that individual is obviously in great distress") rather than negative self-talk ("I'll get even with that S.O.B.; nobody can get away with treating me that way!") and then to find a supportive listener for ventilation of residual feelings.

When modifying the time-out technique for clients with addictive disorders, it is imperative that the relationship between anger and addiction be clearly identified. Clients *must* understand how one factor potentiates negative qualities of the other, or they will fail to establish justifications for affective, cognitive, and behavioral change. One strategy that promotes awareness of this critical connection involves asking clients to assess their patterns of behavior when facing high-risk situations. The anger management-relapse prevention journal (described in Chapter 4) helps clients accomplish this task.

When assessing the suitability of time-out for particular situations, it is important to remind clients that anger is not limited to aggressive responses (actual behaviors intended to harm others) but can also be expressed through social withdrawal, sulking, and other passive responses. The fact that both types of anger generate equally damaging results should also be emphasized. Clients also need reassurance that the time-out technique can be modified to manage both types of anger and can greatly reduce relapse potential if applied on a regular basis.

Resistance to change and denial of personal responsibility for actions and their consequences is a significant barrier that must be overcome when teaching the time-out technique to clients with addictive diseases. Potter-Efron & Potter-Efron (1991a) identify the misdirection of moral anger as one source of this resistance. Appropriate application of moral anger would include expressions of anger to end oppression or unfair practices. Unfortunately, the concept is often misapplied, especially by individuals with rigid, black-and-white thinking. These individuals frequently use moral anger to justify acts of aggression or omission and episodes of substance abuse. Examples of justifications frequently offered to avoid personal responsibility for negative response choices include the following:

- "What if the other person won't cooperate? Do you expect *me* to give in or walk away?"

- "What if the other person is a stranger? It would look pretty stupid if out of the blue I said I need to take a time-out!"
- "How will this help me stay sober? You don't expect me to announce that I need to take a time-out in public—do you?"

In each of the above examples, attempts were made to negate personal responsibility for actions and their consequences. A critical task in teaching time-out to resistant, addicted clients involves instilling the belief that to achieve long-term, quality sobriety you *must* take personal responsibility for, cope with, and redirect feelings and reactions, *regardless* of what the other person may or may not do! The following case examples demonstrate this intervention in action.

CASE STUDY: MR. J.

Mr. J is a 55-year-old, married, employed male with three children between the ages of 10 and 22. His chief complaint is that his spouse constantly berates him for past behavior and refuses to acknowledge the changes he has made. He typically responds by becoming verbally abusive, staying out late, and threatening to drink. The time-out technique was suggested to help Mr. J. avoid the temptation to play into this repetitive cycle of destructive response choices. Mr. J.'s initial reaction was negative, and he snorted, "Nothing has worked so far—why should I put myself through more grief! No matter what I do she just keeps riding me."

Intervention

The initial intervention focused on overcoming Mr. J.'s belief that time-out was a sign of weakness. He was assisted in reframing his thoughts so that time-out could become a strategy for self-empowerment, not surrender. He was encouraged to teach the time-out technique to his wife and seek her support in applying it when he felt angry or unable to respond in a positive manner. The client attempted this approach for several months. He reported that his wife refused to cooperate and was even more abusive when he attempted to engage in time-out. Since the traditional approach failed, Mr. J. was assisted in developing a modified version of time-out. Since this was not a relationship he chose to end, the goal of this intervention became reducing his relapse potential and redirecting anger more constructively. He was instructed to focus on the problem, maintaining sobriety in a highly conflicted environment, not on fault finding. The time-out technique was modified so the client could initiate a cool-off period despite his wife's hostile reactions. When angered, he left the setting, returning when he felt able to respond without becoming aggressive. He always offered to discuss the situation, and if his wife became abusive or resistant, he left the offer open and went on with his own routine.

Outcome

One year postdischarge Mr. J. was contacted to assess the status of his relationship and his sobriety. Although his marital situation remained basically unchanged, he reported more positive relationships with his children and felt this was a direct result of his ability to more constructively express his anger. Most significantly, he had maintained his sobriety! He was praised for his efforts and encouraged to continue this strategy, always leaving the option open for his wife to participate if she chose to.

This case is a good example of an untenable situation that, due to religious convictions, the client felt unable to leave. By teaching him to apply a modified form of time-out, he was able to maintain sobriety and self-control despite the stress in his marriage. Ideally, time-out is a technique for two or more willing players; however, as demonstrated by this case, it *can* work even in the face of strong opposition.

CASE STUDY: MR. S.

Mr. S. is a 43 year-old, married, employed, combat veteran with a history of alcohol dependence and posttraumatic stress disorder. He has a pattern of physical violence followed by alcohol use and blames his victims for his current responses. When discussing the time-out technique as a possible way to redirect his anger and reduce relapse potential, his initial response was "I can't just tell a total stranger I need a time-out! This is a stupid idea!" Mr. S. returned to group the following week and reported that he had become angry with a woman in a grocery store who berated him for having an unmarked item in the express lane. He was unable to contain his anger and resorted to physical violence. He was arrested and charged with assault. Once released on bail, he returned to his home and relapsed. He was shaken by this incident and requested to learn the time-out technique so similar incidents could be prevented.

Intervention

The time-out technique can be successfully applied with strangers in public places with a few modifications. The client was concerned that public announcement of time-out would create more anger than it resolved. He also pointed out that he, like many others confronted with unpleasant situations in public places, had no intention of returning to the setting to resolve the conflict. With these concerns in mind, a modification of the time-out technique was developed. The client was instructed to monitor his behavior and take the following action whenever he felt himself escalating to a point of aggression and/or alcohol use:

1. Silently identify subtle shifts in physical reactions, feelings, thoughts, and behavior which indicate the risk for inappropriate response is escalating.
2. Remind yourself that your feelings and thoughts are becoming unmanageable and you need to take a time-out.
3. Leave the setting quietly, without explanation.
4. Once you are in a safe place, participate in an activity to reduce relapse risk and discharge anger appropriately. Focus on the event, *not* who is at fault. Remind yourself that the incident is *not* personal, even though it feels that way, and that you just happened to be on the receiving end of someone's inappropriate anger.
5. Once you regain a sense of control, praise yourself for avoiding alcohol use and aggressive behavior. You remained in control of your behavior even though the other person did not!
6. Remind yourself that you *cannot* change the behavior of others, but you *can* choose how *you* respond. Also remind yourself that although aggressive responses and alcohol use are still options, the price is high when you choose to activate them.
7. Share this experience with a supportive listener in order to release any residual anger, so it will not be misdirected elsewhere.

Outcome

Contact with this client 6 months after he completed treatment found him coping more effectively with unpleasant situations. He reported that he had experienced multiple high-risk situations since terminating treatment. He went on to report that he had effectively applied the modified time-out technique in all but one instance. In this one situation, he allowed his anger to escalate to aggression; however, he avoided alcohol use following the incident. When asked to explain where the process broke down, he admitted failing to heed the warning signs of increasing anger and passed a point where time-out could be implemented. He used the incident as reinforcement to continue applying time-out and stated he felt less angry with the world and better able to redirect his own behavior in a positive manner.

Mr. S.'s case demonstrates that modified time-outs can be used in any setting. This form of time-out is especially useful when working with clients who feel threatened by relapse and are unable or unwilling to publicly announce their distress. They can silently monitor relapse warning signs and choose to leave the setting before relapse occurs. Once in a safe setting, they can review the event and develop strategies to reduce the likelihood of recurrence.

A second factor contributing to resistance and avoidance of personal responsibility for actions and their consequences is the concept of shame. Potter-Efron and Potter-Efron (1989) identify six defenses used to avoid shame: denial, withdrawal, arrogance, exhibitionism, perfectionism, and rage. Denial and rage are classic responses used by chemically dependent individuals to avoid shame generated by relapse episodes. Because communication is dramatically altered by the dysfunctional family rules "Don't talk, don't trust, don't feel" (Black & Bucky, 1986; Wegscheider, 1981; Wegscheider-Cruse, 1976; Woititz, 1983) anger and other emotions are often suppressed. When negative consequences generated by this lack of communication occur, blame is projected onto others. This pattern of interaction damages relationships and creates a deep sense of shame and powerlessness in the alcoholic/addict. Withdrawal, arrogance (assuming a self-righteous attitude), exhibitionism (acting out by drinking, using drugs, or using anger to control others), and rigid, perfectionistic attitudes and behavior may result, further entrenching this destructive process. Once identified, clients can learn to interrupt this cycle by applying the time-out technique.

CASE STUDY: MS. R.

Ms. R. is a 45-year-old, married, unemployed woman with two children, ages 12 and 15. She was raised in an alcoholic home and uses this experience to justify her own chemical dependence. This client is deeply ashamed of her family history and of her inability to stop using alcohol and cocaine. Multiple failed treatment attempts and five failed marriages contribute to her deep sense of loss and hopelessness. When asked to describe her current relationships, she indicated her husband was threatening to leave and her children had indicated they would go with him if the marriage ended. Her reaction to this confrontation was to become verbally abusive, followed by withdrawal and substance abuse. She expressed a genuine desire to interrupt this process, but her shame and feelings of futility resulted in inaction and the sensation of waiting for the ax to fall.

Intervention

Ms. R. was hospitalized to arrest her addiction and placed in outpatient treatment following discharge. Her family was enrolled in a multifamily group so conflict could be defused. Ms. R. participated in the anger management-relapse prevention training program to develop more effective strategies for expressing anger and other emotions that contributed to relapse episodes. Since her pattern was to "stuff" anger, become verbally abusive once tension escalated beyond a certain point, then resort to substance abuse to alleviate her shame and guilt, the time-out technique was identified as a primary intervention to interrupt this process. Ms. R. was taught to identify triggers and cues that preceded negative response choices. The anger management-relapse prevention journal (Chapter 4) allowed her to target these factors in order to identify when time-out was necessary. Her family was also instructed in the use of time-out and encouraged to support Ms. R. when she activated this technique. She was instructed to take time-out, apply positive self-talk (Chapter 6), and then return to her family and express her feelings and needs using "I" statements and problem solving (Chapters 7 and 8) to accomplish this task.

Outcome

Ms. R. was contacted 1 year after leaving treatment and indicated her situation had stabilized dramatically. She had maintained sobriety and effectively communicated her feelings more than 50% of the time. She admitted that episodes of "stuffing" anger and then becoming verbally abusive still occurred; however, she was more aware of factors that contributed to this process (feeling inadequate or confused; being overtired or pressured) and applied time-out more effectively as opportunities presented themselves. Once shame was identified as the dynamic driving her response choices, she was invited to accept responsibility for existing patterns of response and to challenge the accuracy of her reactions so that more productive response choices could be initiated. Since Ms. R. was motivated to change, time-out produced positive results in her life.

Time-out does not always produce the positive results identified in the preceding case examples. When clients are highly defended, they may be unable to apply this technique and will rationalize that their situation is unique and, therefore, not amenable to time-out. My therapeutic approach is to go with resistance and offer clients every opportunity to define their own treatment outcomes, since continued confrontation only provides fuel for greater resistance and resentment of the therapist's attempt to control their behavior. Since the power of personal change is an inside job, my influence is limited if timing and readiness for change are lacking. Rather than viewing clients in this position as treatment failures, I prefer to define these experiences as mismatched expectations of the therapist and client. I invite clients to return if their position alters, and many eventually cycle through and address their resistance. My hope for those who do not is that they will eventually reach a point of readiness and the interactions we shared may in some small way contribute to a successful outcome.

6

The Role of Self-Talk in the Recovery Process

This chapter revisits a concept introduced in Chapter 3: the influence cognitions exert in determining response choices. An in-depth exploration of the relationship between feelings, cognitions, and response choices, using rational-emotive and cognitive-behavioral approaches as a frame of reference, is the essence of Session 5. Ellis (1962, 1971, 1973, 1985, 1988) , Beck (1976, 1987), and Meichenbaum (1977, 1986) place primary emphasis on the correlation between cognitive process and subsequent emotions and behaviors. They believe that individuals have an innate potential for rational thinking, yet frequently succumb to irrational beliefs. This pattern of faulty thinking stems from childhood, but it is perpetuated through a process of self-suggestion in the here and now (Corey, 1991). Intervention involves a series of cognitive, affective, and behavioral techniques designed to reduce or eliminate self-defeating beliefs that generate emotional disturbance and unproductive response choices.

These approaches are well respected and have produced successful results for many clients; however, they fail to consider the critical role of self-esteem in the recovery process (i.e., my feelings generate cognitions that influence self-esteem and ultimately determine response choices). This is a significant shortcoming, since low self-esteem is a frequent consequence of addiction. When shame, a core feeling for addicts and alcoholics (Potter-Efron & Potter-Efron, 1989), is coupled with the dysfunctional family rules "Don't talk, don't trust, don't feel" (Black & Bucky, 1986; Wegschieder, 1981; Wegscheider-Cruse, 1976; Woititz, 1983), it significantly increases the potential for relapse. If I experience guilt and shame, these emotions generate cognitions that I am worthless or bad, leading to poor self-esteem and episodes of implosive or explosive anger that culminate in relapse. Positive feelings have a similar effect when self-esteem is compromised. If I experience feelings of happiness and success, they generate cognitions such as "I don't deserve to feel so good" or "this just can't last," leading to distortions in self-esteem that promote high-risk behaviors and culminate in relapse.

DiClemente's (1993) transtheoretical model provides a bridge joining the basic tenets of rational-emotive and cognitive-behavioral therapies with my contention that emphasis on self-esteem can produce beneficial rather than the harmful results. DiClemente believes that theories with incompatible explanations regarding the etiology of problem behaviors can be integrated when the focus is on behavior change. An eclectic approach allows for incorporation of divergent concepts without negating the significance of existing theory. Interdependent relationships arising from this union of ideas allow each approach to draw strength from the other, enhancing the overall effectiveness of treatment. This is the rationale behind the material presented in the fifth session. Emphasizing the belief that our thoughts dramatically influence response choices, the primary goal of this session is to teach clients to recognize the potentially negative repercussions of mixing low self-esteem with irrational thoughts.

Counteracting the synergistic effect of low self-esteem and self-defeating cognitions begins with a review of myths perpetuating this dynamic. Primary myths include the following:

- " My emotions are beyond my control. It's too late, I can't change."
- "I have to drink/use to keep my feelings in."
- "I have to drink/use to get my feelings out."
- "My life is so stressful I deserve a drink/fix."
- "What if I change and nobody else is willing to?"
- "If I give up my anger, I will lose face with my peers."

- "I already 'slipped' so I might as well keep drinking/using."
- "I don't deserve to have a better life after what I've done."

Exposing these myths and their damaging effect on self-esteem and the recovery process is critical, since distortions in perceptual set are common for addicts and alcoholics (Annis & Davis, 1987a, 1987b; Gorski & Miller, 1986; Marlatt & Gordon, 1985; Wallace, 1985). Individuals caught in the denial of active addiction develop an unconscious proclivity to repress feelings, distort thoughts, and react impulsively. This unwitting process masks fear, forestalls change, and defers disaster. A dangerous side effect is the irrational belief that "what I refuse to acknowledge does not exist and, therefore, cannot hurt me." Since addiction is a process, consequences may occur weeks, months, or even years after an event, diluting the intensity of cause-and-effect relationships. This delay reinforces denial and discourages the addict/alcoholic from assuming personal responsibility for actions and consequences.

During this session clients explore the irrational nature of current cognitions and identify how the resulting damage to self-esteem generates response choices that perpetuate the anger-relapse cycle. The therapist's challenge is to evoke the realization that we are all ultimately responsible for personal response choices, regardless of what we feel or think or what is occurring in our environment. The rationale that "when events do not go as I planned, I have only one option for response" is challenged and replaced with the view that "events may not always turn out as planned; however, I can learn to recognize the feelings and cognitions that arise from this shift in plans and take action to redirect my response choices." An example will illustrate this concept.

I am flying across the Atlantic to spend a week sightseeing in Paris. I request seating in the nonsmoking section of the plane, since I am highly sensitive to cigarette smoke. After take-off, I discover that I have been assigned a seat in the nonsmoking section directly in front of the first row of smokers. I immediately begin to experience watering eyes and congestion. If I adhere to the belief that I have limited response options, I may choose to suffer in silence and implode my anger. I feel discounted and begin to review other experiences from my past where I felt discounted or ignored. I tell myself that if I were a valued customer, the airline would have honored my seating request or the stewardess would notice my distress and move me to another seat. I continue to suffer in silence, refusing to ask for assistance since the airline *should have known better*. As time passes and my discomfort increases, I rationalize my need to order a drink so I can calm down and avoid becoming verbally abusive to the stewardess and/or the smokers seated directly behind me. Following this relapse, I angrily blame the airline, stating, "If they had seated me as I requested, this never would have happened!" This avoidance of personal responsibility to initiate a change in seating creates a sense of powerlessness, reinforcing the belief that "even if I had spoken up, it wouldn't have changed things anyway." This self-destructive message erodes self-esteem and increases the potential for future relapse episodes.

Approaching this same situation with the revised belief that "I may not always be able to change events but I can change how I feel, think, and respond" generates a very different outcome. I am flying to Paris for a vacation and have requested a nonsmoking seat since I am highly sensitive to cigarette smoke. Soon after take-off I realize I have been placed in a seat directly in front of the first row of smokers. I immediately experience watery eyes and congestion. I feel angry about this situation and become aware of my desire to blame the airline since things are not as they "should be." Instead, I elect to modify my thoughts to reflect the reality: This was an unintentional error and can possibly be corrected. I summon the stewardess and explain my predicament, requesting reassignment to another seat. The stewardess apologizes and takes action to remedy the problem. I feel satisfied that my needs have been acknowledged. The message I give myself, "Things do not always go as planned; however, I do have some control over the outcome if I am willing to identify my needs and request interventions," boosts my self-esteem, reducing my relapse potential.

As demonstrated above, the synergistic effect of low self-esteem and negative cognitions significantly increases the risk of relapse. The remainder of this chapter will focus on teaching clients to identify and modify this self-destructive cycle. Following a review of the myths that fuel this dynamic, clients are introduced to the concept of self-talk. Defined as the chatter that goes on inside our heads as we experience life events, self-talk is identified as a catalyst for change. Because cognitions have the potential to generate both positive and negative interpretations of events, our ability to redirect thoughts can dramatically affect self-esteem and response choices.

Past experiences play a significant role in the evolution of self-esteem and our here-and-now interpretations of life experiences. Clients are referred back to material covered in Session 2 to help them identify this connection. Although causality cannot be assigned, the correlation between past experiences, cognitions, and current response choices lends credibility to the notion of the synergistic relationship described above. Since this review of the past evokes painful memories, clients frequently become resistant, staunchly defending their belief systems and current response choices. A common concern is the fear that challenging core beliefs negates the validity of their lives prior to treatment (i.e., if I determine that I have operated under a set of faulty beliefs all my life, it means everything I have thought, felt, or done is invalid).

To dispel this conviction, clients are reassured that past experiences are both valid and valuable. Because life is a constantly evolving process, thoughts, feelings, and actions that are valid and appropriate in one setting or during a particular stage of life may no longer be valid or appropriate in the here and now. They are invited to evaluate the validity and appropriateness of old feelings and beliefs in their current life and determine which messages need discarding. They are also reminded that negative feelings, self-defeating thoughts, and poor self-esteem are primary relapse triggers, which once identified can be modified to redirect response choices (Annis & Davis, 1987a, 1987b; Ellis et al., 1988; Gorski & Miller, 1986; Marlatt & Gordon, 1985). An exercise designed to identify irrational beliefs, or self-defeating cognitions, contributing to the relapse process helps clients accomplish this task (see Worksheet 4, pp. 172–173).

Clients are given a brief explanation of the worksheet and allowed 10 or 15 minutes to complete the exercise. Group members are then invited to share their discoveries. During this process, comparison of self-defeating thoughts among group members is initiated to target cognitive themes common to individuals in early recovery. The group acts as a barometer for reality testing and an agent for change. As the session unfolds, it is important to provide information regarding the complex nature of beliefs and their influence on our response choices. Four variables contributing to the content of individuals' core beliefs are reviewed to demystify their power:

1. *Past experiences.* When current situations approximate negative experiences from the past, it increases the probability that cognitions and subsequent response choices will reflect hostile, defensive qualities. Conversely, when current situations approximate positive past experiences, it increases the probability that cognitions and subsequent response choices will reflect cooperative, nondefensive qualities.

2. *Self-esteem.* When self-esteem is compromised, individuals are more likely to personalize negative aspects of life experiences and respond inappropriately (i.e., relapse, avoidance, or hostile confrontations). When self-esteem is restored or enhanced, individuals tend to depersonalize negative aspects of life experiences and respond appropriately (i.e., maintain sobriety, activate support networks, and initiate strategies to reduce or eliminate conflict).

3. *Relationships.* The nature of our relationships and their relative state of repair or disrepair significantly influence cognitive interpretations and subsequent response choices. Relationships reflecting a supportive, loving, consistent foundation create positive cognitions and response choices that reflect trust, respect, and cooperative efforts. When they become fragmented, nonsupportive, or antagonistic, cognitions assume a pessimistic or defensive quality and result in response choices reflecting distrust, animosity, and resistance.

4. *Consequences.* When events generate desirable outcomes, feelings, cognitions, and response choices currently in operation are reinforced and repeated when similar situations arise. When events generate painful or undesirable outcomes, feelings, cognitions, and response choices may be modified when similar situations arise (i.e., If I can drink/use, act out, or withdraw and suffer few or no adverse consequences, what motivation do I have to modify my feelings, thoughts, or behavior? If, however, I experience negative consequences when I drink/use, act out, or withdraw, I am much more likely to evaluate my current feelings, thoughts, and behavior to reduce the risk of further negative consequences).

Once these variables are defined, group members participate in an exercise that helps them visually track feelings, thoughts, and response choices along the road to anger and relapse (see Figure 3). They are invited to share personal experiences and identify response choices to increase the potential for positive outcomes in future situations. Role plays provide opportunities for practice applications of this technique. Clients unwilling to participate in this exercise are asked to explore their

Figure 3. Model 3: Choices along the road to anger and relapse.

THE ROAD TO RECOVERY

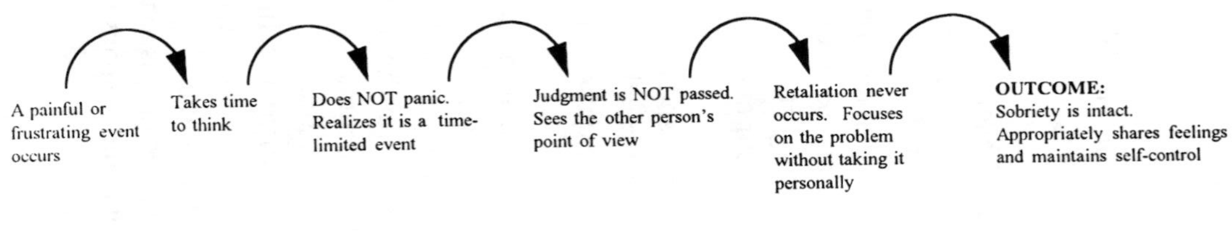

THE ROAD TO RELAPSE

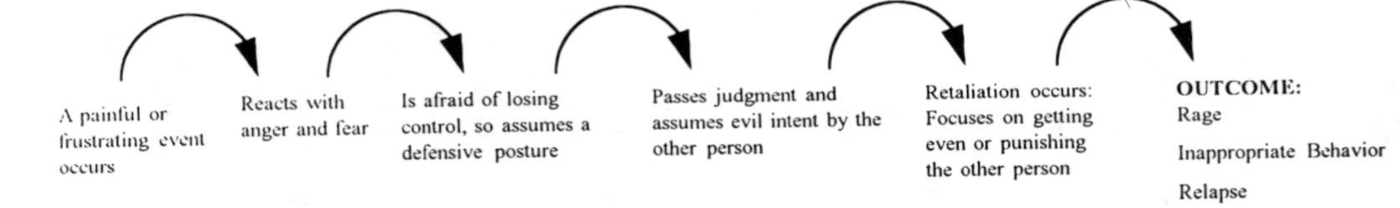

resistance and identify self-defeating thoughts about what participation would mean. Since going with resistance reduces defensiveness, many clients reconsider and join the group process.

A second technique for evaluating current feelings, thoughts, and response choices is the egg timer technique. This intervention, introduced as a homework assignment, allows clients to review their current repertoire from the perspectives of actor and observer. The following instructions are provided when making this assignment:

1. The next time you feel angry or upset, take an egg timer and sit in front of a mirror. Make sure the mirror is in a location free from distractions.
2. Set the egg timer for 5 minutes and proceed to tell yourself *out loud* all the negative feelings and thoughts you are experiencing. Pay special attention to your tone of voice, the gestures and facial expressions you use, and what happens to your anger as this exercise progresses.
3. When 5 minutes has elapsed, reset the timer and replace your negative feelings and thoughts with positive affirmations. Again, notice your tone of voice, the gestures and facial expressions you use, and what happens to your anger.
4. Pay attention to subtle negative cognitions that intrude as you say the affirmations: "This is stupid, I feel like a fool." "What good will this do in the real world?" "I can't believe I'm actually doing this." These thoughts undermine affirmations and reinforce the belief that change is impossible and you are doomed to remain the same miserable person you are now for the rest of your life.
5. At the conclusion of this exercise, write down your feelings, thoughts, and impressions that occurred before, during, and after the exercise and bring the list to group for further discussion.
6. Use this technique as often as necessary. The goal is to increase your awareness of current feelings, thoughts, and response choices and how they affect your recovery.

The egg timer technique is especially useful when clients deny their anger, since it involves visual, auditory, and behavioral observations. Resistance is further eroded because the technique involves self-monitoring. This prevents clients from assuming an external focus and blaming the observer for faulty interpretations because, in this instance, *each client* is the observer!

Detouring self-talk is a difficult technique to teach. Clients frequently sabotage therapists' best efforts to help them modify inappropriate thoughts and behavior. The following case studies demonstrate this therapist's teaching style when detouring self-talk is the recommended intervention.

CASE STUDY: MS. B.

Ms. B. is a 50-year-old, divorced, unemployed white female with a 30-year history of alcohol dependence. She has experienced multiple relapses and blames herself, stating, "I can always seem to pick out my flaws but have a very hard time finding anything good to say about myself." She attempted a variety of treatment interventions during the past 10 years but never achieved more than 3 months of continuous sobriety.

Intervention

Ms. B. was highly motivated to change her behavior since it created painful consequences. She enrolled in the anger management-relapse prevention program, participating in all sessions. Since her primary relapse trigger involved negative self-talk, the focus for intervention occurred during Session 5. Ms. B. completed the irrational thoughts worksheet and kept a diary of her negative thoughts and the triggers stimulating them. The egg timer technique was assigned so she could visualize messages influencing her responses. She was instructed to spend at least 5 minutes daily in front of a mirror giving herself positive affirmations. These affirmations were prepared in advance and placed on note cards to ensure that she remained task oriented. Whenever negative thoughts arose, she was instructed to immediately refute them and insert positive affirmations in their place.

To support her goals of long-term sobriety and a more positive self-image, Ms. B was instructed to attend community-based recovery meetings at least twice weekly. She was encouraged to participate in activities that made her feel productive, and reach out to people who held her in positive regard. A 30-day trial was suggested.

Outcome

At the end of 30 days, Ms. B. reported that she was experiencing a decrease in negative thoughts. She expressed concern despite this improvement because conscious efforts were still needed to dispel negative thoughts. She was reminded that efforts to reinforce the new behaviors were necessary to prevent reactivation of former behaviors. She was reassured that the frequency of reinforcement needed to maintain new responses would gradually decrease, except during periods of distress. During challenging times, daily self-talk exercises and more frequent support group attendance would help sustain sobriety and a positive self-image.

Unfortunately, not all clients are as compliant or motivated as Ms. B. The second example demonstrates application of the self-talk with a resistant client.

CASE STUDY: MR. L.

Mr. L. is a 70-year-old, retired, married male with a 50-year history of alcohol dependence. Multiple relapses mark his long battle to gain sobriety. When asked to define his relapse factors, he stated, "Gee, Jo, I guess I just like to abuse myself!" His usual response, when experiencing strong emotions, involves using criticism and humor to disrupt the flow of interaction. This client has attempted treatment on several occasions, and had participated in my anger management-relapse prevention training program during two prior admissions. The current attempt was precipitated by his wife's declining health and threats of divorce. His demeanor still evidenced denial and resistance. However, this time he was more open, honestly admitting to tactics employed to avert the focus from feelings to thinking.

Intervention

Since Mr. L. was well known to me, he was immediately confronted regarding past behaviors. He was reminded that his current course would remain unchanged until he assumed an active role in the recovery process. Several group members remembered Mr. L. from prior admissions and agreed to confront his smokescreen antics. Mr. L. tested the group on numerous occasions and was surprised that others cared enough to confront him and maintain the focus on his feelings and reactions.

Mr. L. admitted that his relapse pattern appeared to be triggered by feelings of powerlessness and self-doubt. He was asked to recall the detouring self-talk technique he learned during previous admissions. He was also encouraged to repeat the egg timer technique and revise his irrational thoughts worksheet. Mr. L. accomplished these tasks and discovered three irrational beliefs affecting his behavior:

- "I'm too old to change; you can't teach an old dog new tricks."
- "It's too hard to change; I might as well finish the race with the same tired old horse since I'm in the home stretch anyway."
- "I might fail if I try to change, then I'll feel even worse than I already do."

Once these irrational thoughts were identified, Mr. L. was asked to share them in group. After several false starts, group members succeeded in getting him to acknowledge the painful feelings created by these thoughts and to identify how they contribute to his relapse cycle. Time was also spent reviewing his childhood experiences, where many negative thoughts originated. He was encouraged to believe that change is always possible if an individual is willing to experience emotional discomfort as self-defeating thoughts are replaced with productive alternatives.

Mr. L. was instructed to monitor negative self-talk so it could be refuted and replaced with positive affirmations. He attempted this new approach for 6 weeks. Regular progress reports were provided so group support and feedback could sustain his efforts.

Outcome

Six months following treatment, Mr. L. was contacted to assess his progress. Many positive changes were identified. He followed treatment recommendations, successfully using group for feedback to modify negative feelings and self-defeating thoughts. For the first time ever, he acknowledged self-defeating patterns of behavior and took action to modify them. He continues to struggle with painful feelings from past experiences; however, has reached a point of hopefulness and is beginning to see opportunities that were previously unavailable.

In conclusion, I remind you that self-talk also affects therapists! Our perception of progress may drastically differ from that of our clients, and we must continuously monitor our own self-talk so it does not hinder the therapeutic process. Had I allowed my past experiences with Mr. L. to shape my interactions with him during his *third trip* through my training program, I might have unconsciously created roadblocks and impeded his recovery. Remember you are only human—and so are your clients! Practice what you teach and NEVER say NEVER! The unexpected inevitably occurs when you expect it least.

7

Personalizing Responses to Interrupt the Anger-Relapse Cycle

The preceding chapter explored irrational cognitions and helped clients identify how the resulting damage to self-esteem generates response choices that perpetuate the anger-relapse cycle. Emphasis was placed on the need to assume personal responsibility for our response choices, regardless of what we feel or think or what is occurring in here-and-now situations. Building on this concept, Chapter 7 introduces an intervention to help clients personalize responses and interrupt this destructive cycle. Since a primary goal of interpersonal communication is need fulfillment, the ability to accurately and clearly convey our feelings and needs to others is critical. During Session 6 clients are assisted in recognizing how faulty patterns of communication hinder this process. Using the dysfunctional family rules "Don't talk, don't trust, don't feel" (Black & Bucky, 1986; Wegschieder, 1981; Wegscheider-Cruse, 1976; Woititz, 1983) as a frame of reference, the therapist identifies how communications lacking personalized responses lead to power struggles and unproductive outcomes. Failure to identify how I feel, rather than what you have or haven't done, shifts the focus from the problem to who is "right" and who is "wrong." The communication of feelings and needs is lost in this process, and interactions conclude with participants feeling frustrated and discounted. Shifting the blame to others negates personal responsibility for response choices, damaging relationships and escalating relapse potential. Because chemically dependent individuals operate under the influence of dysfunctional family rules, they are especially vulnerable to this unproductive pattern of interaction. The tendency to avoid personal responsibility not only for the expression of feelings and needs but also for the identification and application of strategies to interrupt this process is a major stumbling block in the recovery process. Because successful redirection of anger and relapse urges hinge on the ability to personalize response choices, Session 6 introduces means to accomplish this goal.

The initial task of this session involves teaching clients to identify the three most common avenues of expression people adopt when communicating their feelings, especially anger, to others (Sonkin & Durphy, 1985):

1. "Stuffing" anger to avoid feelings
2. Escalating anger to avoid feelings
3. Directing and openly expressing feelings

To visually depict these avenues, a continuum of response choices is drawn on the board, with stuffing anger at one end, directing anger in the middle, and escalating anger at the opposite end. Clients are informed that behavior never occurs as an isolated event. Behavioral responses exist along a continuum that is influenced by feelings, thoughts, the state of our self-esteem, environmental factors (whom we are with, where we are, what is going on), and our physical condition (well-nourished and rested or deprived of food and sleep). Response choices fluctuate, depending on the constellation of variables present when responses are selected.

Clients inevitably ask, "Jo, I stuff my anger and then end up exploding later down the road. Can a person have more than one pattern of response?" My reply is "Of course! We all have a predominant style for expressing anger and other feelings; however, variations, even extremes, may arise if we encounter situations perceived as threatening, are experiencing negative feelings and thoughts, have poor self-esteem, or are tired and hungry." Individuals whose predominant pattern involves stuffing anger will eventually experience a buildup that may result in explosive outbursts. Individuals who routinely explode anger may retreat in silence following explosive episodes, stuffing anger to avoid further conflict. The goal is to develop a strategy for balancing how we express anger and other feelings so the majority of our communications involve the direct expression of feelings and needs. Failure to accomplish this task will result in extreme responses, increasing relapse potential.

A review of characteristics common to each avenue for expressing feelings, with a focus on anger (see Table 1), assists clients in identifying their predominant pattern of response and the impact these choices have on recovery. Table 1 is written on the board to graphically depict characteristics and consequences of each avenue. Group discussion is actively recruited by the leader during this process. The goal is to help clients conceptualize each avenue and identify potential outcomes when response choices elicit extremes in either direction. The risk of rebounding from one extreme to the other, a consequence of assuming inflexible positions, is also emphasized. Finally, clients are invited to explore the dynamics that lead to extremist behavior as a step toward identifying and reframing the feelings and thoughts that guide current response choices.

Following the discussion of avenues for the expression of anger, group members are encouraged to provide examples so they can practice identifying personal response styles and their potential outcomes. The following examples illustrate this exercise in action.

GROUP EXAMPLE: DINING OUT WITH FRIENDS

You are dining out with a group of friends when someone suggests a round of drinks. Everyone at the table is aware that you are a recovering alcoholic. Think of possible reactions you might experience. What response choices would you select as a stuffer? As an escalator? As a person who directs feelings? (See Table 2 for a sample response choice continuum.)

GROUP EXAMPLE: THE DISBELIEVING SPOUSE

You have been in a recovery program for 6 months and are maintaining your sobriety. Despite this progress, your spouse continues to question

Table 1
The Three Most Common Avenues for Expressing Anger

Stuffing Anger	Escalating Anger	Directing Anger
Swallows feelings	Hostile and demanding	Focuses on personal reactions
Avoids healthy confrontation	Spews emotions randomly	Openly expresses feelings
Hoards resentments as ammunition for the future	Uses aggression and intimidation to get own way	Focuses on the problem
Blames others for not figuring out the "right" response	Blames others when things go wrong	Avoids blaming others when things go wrong
		Gets point across and remains realistic: Realizes he or she won't always get own way
Resorts to substance abuse and other forms of self-destructive behavior	Resorts to substance abuse and incites conflict	Avoids substance abuse and other forms of self-destructive behavior
Deprives the other person of the right to respond	Refuses to consider the other person's point of view	Allows the other person an opportunity to respond
Consequences	**Consequences**	**Consequences**
High relapse potential	High relapse potential	Reduced relapse potential
Creates social isolation	Creates social isolation	Reduces social isolation
Estranges partners	Damages relationships	Restores relationships
Prevents problem resolution	Impedes problem resolution	Enhances problem resolution
Low self-esteem	Low self-esteem	Improved self-esteem
Feels powerless	Feels helpless and ashamed	Has a sense of control
May lead to explosive behavior or withdrawal and regression	Generates fear and erodes trust	Reduces tension

Table 2
Response Choice Continuum from Group Example: Dining Out with Friends

A stuffer would . . .	An escalator would . . .	A director would . . .
Refrain from expressing how vulnerable he or she feels around alcohol	Become hostile and demand that friends refrain from drinking in his or her presence	Openly express discomfort
Make an excuse and leave	Launch an attack to create a distraction	Request that friends refrain from alcohol use, but neither demand nor sulk
Make indirect comments, hoping someone will guess his or her feelings and intervene	Storm out, slinging obscenities	Explain that if he or she begins to experience urges to drink, he or she may have to leave abruptly
Participate in alcohol use and silently blame friends	Use friends' behavior as an excuse to drink, and then blame them for the relapse incident	Assume responsibility for own sobriety. Avoid using friends' behavior as an excuse for relapse
Feel used and abused. Use this incident as an excuse to withdraw from recovery	Feel out-of-control and overwhelmed. Use this incident to justify further alcohol use	Take an active role in planning the next outing in an alcohol-free environment
HIGH RISK FOR RELAPSE	HIGH RISK FOR RELAPSE	MAINTAINS SOBRIETY!!!

your sobriety. Today you were 15 minutes late getting home from work and were accused of drinking. What response choices would you select as a stuffer? As an escalator? As a person who directs feelings? (See Table 3 for a sample response choice continuum.)

These group exercises reinforce the idea that the open and direct expression of feelings generates a sense of self-control, while stuffing and escalating exacerbates existing problems. Since clients actively participate in creating the responses for each category, they have opportunities to compare their own behavior to behavior illustrated in group examples. This provides a nonthreatening avenue for self-exploration that facilitates the awareness necessary for future change.

Table 3
Response Choice Continuum from Group Example: The Disbelieving Spouse

A stuffer would . . .	An escalator would . . .	A director would . . .
Feel hurt and angry but avoid expressing these emotions to their partner	Become defensive and verbally abusive. May resort to physical violence if spouse's behavior continues	Attempt to share feelings focusing on how THEY feel rather than on what the other person did wrong
Withdraw or use outside activities to escape	Act self-righteous and accuse the other person of attempting to sabotage their recovery	Invite their partner to share reactions so they can understand the other person's point of view
Act "Funny" but insist everything is fine	Refuse to consider the other person's feelings or discuss factors that precipitate attacks. Feel slighted and hopeless	Attempt to settle the present issue without dragging in history
Brood and feel sorry for themself—may resort to substance abuse and then blame their partner for "making them do it"	May use this as an excuse to use substances and act out, blaming their partner for the consequences	Avoid counter-attacks regardless of their partner's actions
Indirectly express feelings using smoke-screens and passive-aggressive behavior then deny everything if confronted	Use hostility to build fences around themself and refuse to address the problem head-on	State what they would like to have happen in the relationship and offer a compromise to resolve the issue
HIGH RISK FOR RELAPSE	HIGH RISK FOR RELAPSE	MAINTAINS SOBRIETY!!!

"I" MESSAGES

Once this initial task has been accomplished, the inevitable question comes up: "Jo, we know that open and direct expression of our feelings is the best thing to do, but *how do we do it*?" The session becomes more didactic at this juncture, and clients are tutored in the art of using "I" messages (Deschner, 1984). They are instructed to follow these simple rules when applying "I messages":

1. Identify the *specific behavior* that creates your reaction.
2. Clearly state *how you feel* about the behavior.
3. Define *the reason* you feel the way you do.
4. *Ask for* what you would like to experience in future interactions.

Example: When you ____________, I feel __________________ because ___________________. What I would like is ____________.

To further justify the use of "I" messages, a brief explanation of why they seem to work is provided. Clients learn that "I" messages place emphasis on the sender rather than the receiver, creating a vehicle for the nondefensive expression of feelings. In addition, "I" messages focus on feelings without blaming or judging, increasing the likelihood of positive outcomes. Finally, explaining the reason for specific feelings and offering alternatives for the future promotes cooperative efforts.

Despite the power "I" messages allegedly possess, clients generally resist learning them and offer a variety of excuses:

- "Come on Jo—that sounds so stupid! People would laugh me out of the room!"
- "I tried something like that before and it only made matters worse!"
- "I don't have time to memorize this junk! I have enough trouble expressing myself without complicating things!"

When this dynamic comes into play, the therapist must move quickly. Group members are encouraged to participate in role plays to minimize self-consciousness and reinforce new skills. Humor is another critical element in the teaching process. When clients laugh with each other while learning new skills, they are more willing to take these skills home and implement them—especially if encouraged to return the following week and process the consequences.

Clients should be warned that a "honeymoon" reaction, followed by a backlash of anger, may be experienced as they apply this new intervention. The importance of understanding that years of friction will not magically disappear with the introduction of "I" messages is critical to prevent clients from prematurely discarding the technique. Significant others frequently act out more intensely during initial shifts in clients' behavior because they are afraid to believe the change is real. They also fear manipulation. In a relationship involving an addicted partner, *all* change is viewed with suspicion because experience has led the nonaddicted partner to expect the worst. Clients are encouraged to *consistently* apply "I" messages, invite their significant others to participate in practice sessions, and view acting out behaviors as part of the recovery process. The following examples demonstrate "I" messages in action.

CASE STUDY: MR. AND MRS. G.

Mr. and Mrs. G. enrolled in treatment following a marital crisis precipitated by Mr. G.'s alcohol use and aggressive behavior. Mr. G. was 47-years-old and Mrs. G. was 45-years-old. The marriage faced dissolution unless Mr. G. arrested his alcoholism and the couple repaired their damaged relationship. Both identified a pattern of escalating conflict, and neither knew how to appropriately express feelings so explosive altercations could be avoided. When asked to state their expectations of treatment, they both replied "sobriety and a happier marriage."

Intervention

Since this couple was motivated, information about addiction and recovery was introduced. In the multifamily group they focused on sharing feelings and learned to confront each other using "I" messages. Group support during these encounters greatly enhanced their confidence and encouraged them to explore a number of issues in their relationship. Mr. G. worked concurrently in the anger management-relapse prevention group, exploring his tendency to stuff anger and later become explosive. Since he felt intimidated by his spouse's superior verbal skills, role plays were used to help him practice responses before sharing them in multifamily group. The G.'s were instructed to practice "I" messages in conjunction with time-out when conflict became unmanageable. Each week they processed their experiences in group.

Outcome

As the G.'s approached termination, they acknowledged improvement in defusing hostility and resolving disagreements. Mr. G. reported feeling more equal in the relationship and sheepishly admitted his tendency to project blame and use this as an excuse to relapse. The couple voiced concerns that they would revert to old patterns of behavior once treatment ended. They were encouraged to apply new skills on a daily basis to reduce the risk of regression.

When the couple concluded treatment they were making good progress, and Mr. G. had maintained his sobriety for a year. Since both were motivated and willing to compromise, long-term positive results are anticipated. Not all cases follow such a smooth course, as will be demonstrated below.

CASE STUDY: THE M. FAMILY

Mr. M. was a 40-year-old, married, unemployed, alcohol-dependent client. He has been married 14 years and has three children, ages 13, 11, and 7. The family entered treatment to help Mr. M. sustain sobriety after discharge from a 28-day inpatient program. Family members were hostile and defensive, blaming Mr. M. for all their problems. He in turn threatened relapse if family pressures continued. All five family members attended multifamily group, and Mr. M. concurrently attended the anger management-relapse prevention group. Their initial goals were for Mr. M. to maintain sobriety and for the family to improve interpersonal relationships.

Intervention

The M.'s displayed typical characteristics of an addicted family system: an inability to openly share feelings and resolve disputes. Mr. M.'s alcohol dependence created an imbalance in family responsibilities, with the burden of care falling on Mrs. M. The children were forced into parentified roles to support Mom and protect Dad from relapse. These factors generated deep-seated resentments, placing family members in antagonistic roles.

Several strategies were employed to disrupt this pattern. First, family members learned to identify self-defeating patterns of interaction. Didactic instruction and role plays were used to accomplish this task. They were instructed to use "I" messages to express displeasure, since current behaviors prevented meaningful communication. Mr. M., like Mr. G. in the preceding example, practiced "I" messages concurrently in the anger management-relapse prevention group to reinforce appropriate responses. He learned to avoid negative reactions when baited by family members and developed a pattern of *consistently* responding with time-out, detouring self-talk, and "I" messages.

Outcome

Predictably, Mr. M.'s family became even more caustic during early phases of treatment. He reported an increase in blaming and shaming by all family members, especially his wife and 7-year-old son. He was encouraged to confront family members in multifamily group so issues could be addressed with the support of a therapist and other families. The client followed these recommendations and reported that following this confrontation his family began to respond more positively, sharing past resentments and current fears. This breakthrough was shared in group and generated positive feelings for all family members. Although Mr. M. was initially skeptical due to family resistance, he complied with treatment recommendations and was pleasantly surprised by the outcome.

The preceding examples demonstrate successful application of "I" messages. Unfortunately, there are instances when clients cannot elicit support and continue to experience distress in intimate relationships. In these situations clients must learn that although they cannot control the responses of others, they *can* control their own responses.

If efforts to elicit change or diminish conflict fail, clients must decide whether relationships contribute more than they cost in terms of happiness and sobriety. They are also reminded that "I" messages enhance the potential for successful outcomes but provide no guarantees. Since "I" messages are frequently applied in conjunction with time-out and detouring self-talk, clients are encouraged to actively combine skills to maximize their chance of a successful outcome. The fact that nothing works all the time is emphasized, to avoid a "sour grapes" response. Finally, clients are reassured that the anger management-relapse prevention training program identifies a number of interventions, so if one fails, another might be successful. The following chapter will present the use of problem solving as a relapse prevention tool.

8

Problem Solving as a Relapse Prevention Strategy

Chapter 8 introduces a technique designed to reframe the concept of conflict and provides an alternative approach for resolving internal (incongruence in one's beliefs and actions) and interpersonal (inconsistencies in the beliefs and actions of two or more people) dissonance. Introduction of this material in Session 7 often generates resistance, since clients with substance abuse disorders frequently adopt a fatalistic outlook on life. Past experiences (e.g., lost relationships, employment difficulties, inability to arrest an addiction) foster the belief "I have little control over events in my life." Negative feelings roused by these encounters and fed with self-defeating cognitions erode self-esteem, creating an attitude of hopelessness and helplessness. Ensuing apathy further reinforces the belief that "things will never change," creating a vicious cycle of half-hearted attempts, repeated failure, social withdrawal, and relapse.

To promote the validity of problem solving as an effective relapse prevention tool, the therapist begins Session 7 by reviewing the role irrational beliefs play in current response choices and their consequent outcomes (material first presented in Sessions 2 and 3). Clients are reminded that irrational beliefs are perpetuated by autosuggestion and self-repetition in the here and now (Ellis, 1962, 1971, 1973, 1985, 1987a;

Ellis & Becker, 1982; Ellis & Bernard, 1984, 1985; Ellis & Grieger, 1977, 1986; Ellis & Harper, 1975). Because self-statements and subjective interpretation of life experiences directly impact outcomes in contemporary situations, the potential for change exists, *if* we are willing to modify existing cognitions (Beck, 1987; DeRubeis & Beck, 1988; Meichenbaum, 1977, 1986). Since feelings of hopelessness and helplessness interfere with this process, the next step involves reframing the concept of powerlessness.

Wallace (1985) applies an interesting twist to the concept of powerlessness. This term is generally perceived as negative or bad. Being powerless means you are not in control and have little or no opportunity to influence outcomes. Wallace challenges this perception, offering a provocative alternative: powerlessness as a stepping-stone to health. According to Wallace, if we stop struggling and accept current situations, negative energy can be directed toward productive recovery efforts. This means when we face undesirable outcomes (relapse, inability to achieve a desired goal) energy normally used to produce negative feelings and thoughts can be redirected into more productive activities (arresting the relapse, redefining goals). If an event cannot be altered, the development of more rational attitudes about the event is essential, so problem solving skills can be successfully applied (Ellis & Dryden, 1987; Ellis et al., 1988). The need to establish *realistic goals* (i.e., what constitutes a reasonable outcome, given all the variables involved in specific situations) is equally important, since unrealistic goals will sabotage the problem-solving process.

Even when clients agree with the above assumptions, a second, equally challenging task remains before the problem-solving technique can be introduced. Clients frequently express the belief that conflict should be avoided at all cost. This belief emanates from the dysfunctional family rules "Don't talk, don't trust, don't feel" (Black & Buckey, 1986; Wegscheider, 1981; Wegscheider-Crus, 1976; Woititz, 1983). These unwritten rules governed family patterns of communication and served the purpose of maintaining the status quo. Conflict was perceived as threatening, since even minimal shifts in existing patterns of interaction resulted in chaotic instability. After identifying this connection, clients are invited to contemplate the possibility that conflict, when handled appropriately, can inoculate them against relapse and create pathways to healthy interaction.

Conflict, they are advised, occurs when opposition exists *between* two or more people, or *within* an individual experiencing dissonance between actions and beliefs. When individuals are unable to achieve desired goals or resolve discrepancies between actions and beliefs, conflict arises. Although conflict is a normal and necessary part of healthy relationships, most people have no idea how to constructively approach and resolve it. Therefore, a primary objective at this point in the session involves teaching clients the difference between unproductive dissidence (the conflict model) and productive dissent (the problem-solving model). This is accomplished in a group exercise that identifies characteristics of each model, then invites clients to place themselves accordingly (see Table 4).

This exercise is followed by an in-depth description of the problem-solving model. Clients are invited to view the model as a foundation upon which to build patterns of expressing and resolving issues. An analogy is used to illustrate this point. When constructing a house, builders refer to blueprints, making modifications when needed to assure the resulting structure is sound. Attempts to shortcut steps or use inferior materials result in an unstable structure. The process of approaching conflict is very similar. One must follow a carefully developed plan of action and be willing to apply modifications, when needed, to form predictable patterns of interaction and promote positive outcomes.

Clients generally express skepticism at this point, stating, "Jo, people don't always cooperate! This will never work in my situation!" Another common criticism is "My biggest problem is me! Are you telling me I can problem solve issues I have with myself?" Their incertitude is acknowledged by the therapist, and they are encouraged to reserve judgment until the session's conclusion. A review of steps necessary to engage the problem-solving model (see Worksheet 5, pp. 174–175) is followed by practice applications of the model.

Following group discussion of Worksheet 5, the leader offers an example of the problem-solving model in action. This example demonstrates successful application of the model by a group of hospitalized psychiatric patients. The purpose of sharing this story is to generate optimism that if the technique can be applied successfully in a restricted environment, it might also be effective for participants in the current group.

Table 4
Models of Conflict Resolution

The Conflict Model	The Problem-Solving Model
Adversarial roles are assumed	Is egalitarian in nature
Positions demarcating "right" and "wrong" are drawn between adversaries	Positions of cooperative efforts, compromise, and negotiations are assumed by participants
Problems are NOT clearly defined and efforts to express feelings are openly defied	Problems ARE clearly defined at the onset so competing interests will not interfere with the issue at hand
The communication process breaks down as participants assume defensive postures and negate points of view that differ from their own	The expression of feelings and views is encouraged so participants can better understand each other's position, enhancing the communication process
Transactions are in the form of threats and demands	Transactions are in the form of requests or statements
The goal is to "win" or prove one's point, regardless of the cost to other parties involved	The goal is to maximize the potential of positive outcomes for all parties involved so everyone comes out a winner
Creates a one-up, one-down situation where there is a clear winner and loser	Supports equal value of participants, preventing the assignment of a winner and loser
Leads to increasing tension, resentment, and hostility. Acts of revenge are common	Leads to decreasing tension, resentment, and hostility. Acts of revenge seldom occur
The end result is unmet needs of all parties involved	The end result is that all participants generally achieve at least part of their desired goal

CASE PRESENTATION BY GROUP LEADER

Participants in this problem-solving exercise were patients on a locked acute care psychiatric unit. Most were hospitalized for exacerbation of psychiatric symptoms (florid symptoms of schizophrenia, manic episodes, and depression with suicidal or homicidal ideations). Due to the severity of their illnesses, patients were confined to the ward until stabilized, at which time they received privilege cards to leave the unit for brief periods. Their primary source of contact with the outside world during this probationary period was two pay phones on the unit. These pay phones were notorious for breakdowns, and repair crews responded slowly to requests for maintenance.

During an educational class explaining the problem-solving technique, clients reported that staff members discounted their complaints regarding chronic telephone problems. Individuals who did openly attempt to resolve this problem were often referred to as "agitated" or "psychotic." As the unit social worker at the time, I offered to help clients develop a strategy for resolving this problem. Although skeptical, they patiently listened as I outlined the problem-solving model. The more lucid clients expressed interest, so a group problem-solving exercise ensued.

PROBLEM

Pay phones on a locked psychiatric unit are chronically broken isolating new clients from the outside world.

POSSIBLE SOLUTIONS

1. Pull the phones out of the wall.
2. Blow up the hospital.
3. Storm the director's office to complain.
4. Use the social worker's phone.
5. Write letters.
6. Use the conference room phone.
7. Appoint a spokesperson to speak to the chief psychiatrist.

PROS AND CONS OF SUGGESTED SOLUTIONS

1. Pulling phones out of the wall would further delay repairs.
2. Blowing up the hospital would mean clients have nowhere to go when psychotic and needing care.
3. Storming the director's office would create chaos and scare people, making it unlikely that their problem would be addressed.
4. There were 40 clients on the ward and only one social worker—not enough time in the day for this option.

5. Some clients were too sick to write, and replies would take days to receive.
6. Since this room was rarely in use, and always monitored by a nurse, it might be an option for clients without privilege cards.
7. Since the social worker is the liaison between clients and staff, this person might best represent clients' needs to the chief psychiatrist.

BEST SOLUTION OR COMBINATION OF SOLUTIONS

After reviewing benefits and consequences of potential solutions, clients elected to discard solutions 1–5 and focus on developing a plan to activate solutions 6 and 7.

PLAN OF ACTION

Target Dates: **Start:** Within 24 hours
Monitor Results: Within 72 hours

Have unit social worker approach the chief psychiatrist and explain the problem and its impact on new patients. Request permission for clients *without privilege cards* to access the conference room phone for 5 minutes per person per day until the pay phones are repaired. Privilege-card holders would use pay phones outside the unit to avoid overloading this system.

REVIEW AND PRAISE EFFORTS

This plan was reviewed with the chief psychiatrist following the problem-solving session. He agreed, implementing it immediately. The social worker informed clients of the outcome, and they congratulated each other on a job well done!

PROBLEM AREAS FOR ADDITIONAL ACTION

NONE

After this presentation, group members are generally willing to give the model a try. A request for volunteers is made and, of course, everyone looks at the floor! I use humor to defuse the tension, and inevitably someone sheepishly volunteers to share an issue. The first case study illustrates application of the model to a problem involving another person, and the second case study demonstrates steps for resolving conflict within oneself.

CASE STUDY: FAMILY VERSUS SOBRIETY

Mr. D. is a 40-year-old, married, employed male with a 20-year history of alcohol dependence. His family of origin drinks heavily, and several members are actively drinking alcoholics. Mr. D., sober for 6 months, has been invited to attend a family reunion in his home state. He knows alcohol will flow liberally and is torn between his desire to rekindle family ties and to protect his newfound sobriety.

PROBLEM

Client desires to maintain sobriety while attending a family reunion that presents high relapse potential.

POSSIBLE SOLUTIONS

1. Decline the invitation and make an excuse.
2. Tell the family he can only attend if they agree not to drink.
3. Attend and carry a wine bottle filled with soda so people will think he is drinking.
4. Tell everyone he has a bleeding ulcer and can't drink.
5. Openly address his recovery with family members and develop contingency plans in case he begins to feel the urge to drink.
6. Locate an AA meeting in his home state which he can attend while visiting.
7. Initiate Antabuse therapy briefly as an extra safeguard.

PROS AND CONS OF SUGGESTED SOLUTIONS

1. This solution is simply avoiding the issue, which may create hard feelings. Further, what will happen the next time an invitation is extended?
2. Since alcohol is an integral part of all family functions, and the event is not being held in his home, he has little control over the behavior of others. His insistence on abstinence will generate a wall of resistance.
3. This solution is also a bad option because this behavior of "romancing the bottle" is one step away from relapse and entrenches denial of his disease.
4. This option is another form of denial and rationalization, which will inevitably lead to relapse.
5. Client can take responsibility for his own behavior and avoid shifting the focus to others. By developing contingency plans, he can protect his sobriety while preserving the right of others to drink, if that is their desire.
6. AA is a good safety net for ventilating feelings appropriately if things start getting sticky.
7. This solution is a good reminder that alcohol is NOT an option.

BEST SOLUTION OR COMBINATION OF SOLUTIONS

A review of options by group members led this client to discard solutions 1–4. He elected to concurrently apply solutions 5, 6, and 7 to increase his potential of preserving his sobriety without foregoing the reunion.

PLAN OF ACTION

Target Dates: **Start:** Within 2 days
Monitor Results: First group session following the reunion

The client's plan involved these steps:

1. Meet with the clinic physician and implement Antabuse therapy.
2. Locate an AA meeting and plan to attend as a visiting member.

3. Contact family members; discuss concerns and advise them of these plans so hard feelings can be avoided.
4. Reserve a hotel room so an alcohol-free setting is available should cravings arise.
5. Secure an open-ended airline ticket in case the risk of relapse becomes so intense that immediate departure is essential.

REVIEW AND PRAISE EFFORTS

Following the reunion, Mr. D. shared his experience with the group. He successfully maintained his sobriety and attended the entire reunion. To his amazement, family members were supportive, and several admitted fears regarding their own drinking patterns. He stayed with a sister who abstained from drinking, enhancing family ties. Although he did not attend an AA meeting, it was reassuring to know this option existed. Antabuse was a good intervention since the one time he experienced cravings it prevented him from ingesting alcohol. He felt very positive about the experience and received positive feedback from the group.

PROBLEM AREAS FOR ADDITIONAL ACTION

Mr. D. felt the only improvement to this plan would have been to implement it 10 years sooner.

CASE STUDY: THE SELF-INFLICTED RELAPSE CYCLE

Mr. Z. is a 55-year-old, employed, divorced male with five failed marriages and multiple suicide attempts. His worst relapse trigger was negative thinking, which inevitably led to relapse and suicidal ideations. Mr. Z. expressed a desire to problem solve this issue, stating, "I've tried everything else—what do I have to lose!"

PROBLEM

Client's pattern of destructive self-talk perpetuates relapse and suicidal ideations.

POSSIBLE SOLUTIONS

1. Commit suicide and stop the cycle once and for all.
2. Accept that it's too late to change and get used to living with things the way they are.
3. See a doctor and get tranquilizers to numb emotional pain.
4. Go through psychoanalysis to discover the root of the problem.
5. Develop a plan to short-circuit negative thoughts and replace them with constructive alternatives.

PROS AND CONS OF SUGGESTED SOLUTIONS

1. A permanent solution that shuts out all other possibilities.
2. A pessimistic point of view, since change is always possible when a desire to evoke shifts in one's behavior is present.
3. Only addresses symptoms, so the problem will continue to surface when medication is discontinued.
4. Although a possibility, this form of therapy requires a long-term time investment and considerable sums of money—both unacceptable options for this client.
5. Would place the client in control of the decision-making process helping him to escape self-induced victimization.

BEST SOLUTION OR COMBINATION OF SOLUTIONS

A review of the options eliminated solutions 1–4 within five minutes. This left option 5 which Mr. Z. felt might work.

PLAN OF ACTION

Target Dates: **Start:** The day following group
Monitor Results: In 30 days

The client's plan involved these steps:

1. Track patterns of negative self-talk by carrying a small notepad to record thoughts as they occur.
2. After tracking destructive thoughts for 1 week, consciously apply time-out and positive self-talk to disrupt this process.

3. Update group members weekly regarding progress and problem areas so modifications can be initiated.

REVIEW AND PRAISE EFFORTS

When the 30-day trial ended, Mr. Z. had identified a core of negative thoughts that activated self-destructive behavior. Most arose from messages received during childhood and focused on his worth and intelligence. Once identified, he countered with these competing thoughts: "I accepted these messages; I can choose to reject them. I am intelligent and valuable. My past *does not* determine my future!"

PROBLEM AREAS FOR ADDITIONAL ACTION

Mr. Z. felt this plan was working but admitted he needed further reinforcement to move beyond a lifetime of defeatist thinking. He added the following modifications to the original plan:

1. Continue to record thoughts in the anger management-relapse prevention journal. When negative thoughts increase, request additional support from staff and group members.
2. Locate an AA club and secure a sponsor.
3. Cultivate friendships so support is available during times of stress.
4. Practice applying positive affirmations daily. Remember that behavior change requires a lifetime commitment.
5. Enroll in the anger process group (discussed in Chapter 14) to address unresolved issues.

Follow-Up

Mr. Z. was contacted 6 months postdischarge to assess his status. He reported compliance with all modifications to his original plan. He was still sober and felt optimistic more than despondent. Periods of melancholy occasionally arose, but he felt better equipped to counteract these moods with skills acquired in the anger management-relapse prevention program.

Mr. D. and Mr. Z. both experienced positive results by applying the problem-solving model. Not everyone is this fortunate, however, so Session 7 concludes with the following observations:

1. Problem solving is *not* a panacea. The goal is to increase positive outcomes when conflict arises; however, *there are no guarantees!*
2. Others will not always cooperate, even when our intentions are honorable. In these instances, problem solving functions as a tool to promote self-control and prevent regressive responses.
3. In some cases, we refuse to cooperate with ourselves! Awareness that a catalyst for change exists when we *do* reach a state of readiness accelerates recovery.
4. A clear and concise description of the problem is *critical* to successful application of this model!
5. The development of an action plan, complete with step-by-step details for its implementation, is vital. Shortcuts create unhappy endings.

When teaching the problem-solving model to clients with addictive diseases, three primary goals are paramount: challenging the dysfunctional family rules that generate negative feelings and self-defeating cognitions, providing alternative strategies to prevent implosion and explosion of anger, and identifying an avenue of empowerment to bolster self-esteem and interrupt the anger-relapse cycle. Although these goals are initiated during this session, clients often need additional information regarding their current style of communication to effectively apply the problem-solving model. Chapter 9 provides an in-depth exploration of this issue.

9

Identifying Current Styles of Communication

Effective communication skills form the building blocks for successful interpersonal relationships. Unfortunately, most clients with substance abuse histories function under the dysfunctional family rules "Don't talk, don't trust, don't feel" (Black & Bucky, 1986; Wegscheider, 1981; Wegscheider-Crus, 1976; Woititz, 1983). These rigid, unwritten rules impose the belief that stuffing feelings, or masking them with explosive reactions, creates an invisible shield behind which one can endure the trauma of active addiction. If we evade intimacy, avoid revealing our vulnerabilities, sidestep the identification of feelings and needs, and fail to develop boundaries distinguishing personal zones of comfort and discomfort, we can maintain a sense of safety behind this uncomfortably familiar cloak of addictive denial. An unfortunate consequence is activation of the anger-relapse cycle. Constructed from negative feelings, self-defeating thoughts, low self-esteem, and inadequate coping skills, the resulting concoction creates a synergistic effect that significantly increases relapse potential.

This destructive process places addicts and alcoholics at a distinct disadvantage when they attempt to engage in interpersonal relationships. Living behind the shield of addictive denial creates severe distortions in one's feelings, thoughts, and self-image. It also distorts interpretations involving the feelings and actions of others. The inability to perceive one's role in creating, and therefore modifying, feelings, cognitions, and outcomes leads to withdrawal from all who dare to question current patterns of response. The dysfunctional family rules further exacerbate this dilemma by preventing the addict/alcoholic from approaching others to assess the accuracy of his or her interpretations.

Limited insight regarding their role in the persistence of negative feelings and self-defeating patterns of thinking and behaving traps substance abusers in a cycle of reaction-rejection-withdrawal-relapse. As pointed out in earlier chapters, interactions with self (self-talk) and interpretations of life experiences greatly influence our feelings, thoughts, and behavior (Annis, 1986; Annis & Davis, 1987a, 1987b; Beck, 1976, 1988; Beck et al., 1979; Daley, 1988; Ellis, 1973, 1985; Ellis & Becker, 1982; Ellis & Dryden, 1987; Ellis & Greiger, 1977; Ellis & Harper, 1975; Ellis et al., 1988; Ellis & Whiteley, 1979; Mahoney, 1974; Mahoney & Thoresen, 1974; Marlatt & Gordon, 1985; Meichenbaum, 1977; Walen et al., 1980; Wessler & Wesler, 1980). Using the work of DiClemente (1993) to bridge theoretical differences, I add the contention that self-esteem also plays a significant role in response choices. Therefore, a prerequisite for recovery involves recognition and mollification of triggers and cues that elicit high-risk feelings, thoughts, and behaviors. The acquisition of this skill is neither swift nor easy; therefore, repetition is the most judicious form of intervention. Reframing materials presented during earlier sessions, Session 8 offers a fresh new look at the communication process and its impact on recovery

The first step in this process involves teaching clients to identify personal styles of communication. The concept of behavior occurring along a continuum is emphasized. Our style of communication may vary, contingent upon whom we are with; what we are feeling, thinking, and doing; when it is occurring; where we are physically located; how the event transpired; and why this, why now. Although it is important to stress the potential for deviation, it is equally important to stress that each of us has a predominant style of communication that dictates how we interact with ourselves and others. Learning to recognize our own unique style, and the variations that arise when we are stressed, tired, angry, confused, or scared, creates opportunities to modify response choices as events unfold.

Following this introduction, clients are introduced to four vehicles through which individuals activate feelings, thoughts, and behavior:

1. *Emphatic communications:* A response style characterized by identification of feelings and needs and honest feedback regarding the desired outcome of a specific interaction or event
2. *Acquiescent communications:* A response style characterized by avoidance of feelings and failure to communicate desired outcomes of specific interactions or events
3. *Combative communications:* A response style characterized by hostile, aggressive expression of feelings that violates the rights of others. Desired outcomes of specific interactions or events are expressed in the context of black-and-white thinking, and input from others is rejected.
4. *Passive-Explosive communications:* A response style characterized by avoidance of feelings, followed by a buildup of resentment that culminates in hostile or aggressive responses. The resulting confusion occludes the ability to effectively convey desired outcomes of specific interactions or events.

Since many clients identify both intrapsychic and interpersonal conflict as primary relapse triggers, it is crucial for them to recognize their role in this process, so unproductive response choices can be modified. The inference of personal responsibility for contributing to *and* resolving sources of conflict generally meets with hearty resistance. Clients with addictive disorders are experts in assigning blame to others, and the idea that *their* feelings, thoughts, and behavior could in any way create or exacerbate negative consequences astonishes them. Since this concept is unfamiliar and threatens existing beliefs, a frequent response is defensive rationalization: "Come on, Jo, do you really expect me to believe that if I change how I think and act things might be different! Why don't you join the real world."

To counteract this resistance, an exercise designed to identify communication styles is enlisted (see Table 5). Clients are invited to identify current response styles and evaluate whether change is needed. Defensive responses such as "Give me a break! You're telling me I can never curse or hit anyone again?" are met with the reassurance that current response choices do not have to change *unless* the individual wants

Table 5
Primary Vehicles in the Communication Process

Emphatic Communication	Acquiescent Communication	Combative Communication	Passive-Explosive Communication
Is self-enhancing	Is self-denying	Is self-enhancing at the expense of others	Is self-denying at the expense of others
Openly shares feelings and needs	Cloisters feelings and needs	Aggressively identifies feelings and needs	Disguises feelings, then blames others for not correctly identifying them
Chooses for self	Allows others to choose for him or her	Chooses for others	Allows others to choose, then reneges
Is straightforward in expressing dissatisfaction when differences occur	Is circumstantial in expressing dissatisfaction when differences occur	Violates the feelings and rights of others when differences occur	Blows smokescreens when expressing dissatisfaction, confusing others
Avoids resentments, since feelings are not allowed to fester unspoken	Reduces the potential for achieving desired goal	Achieves desired goal by hurting others	Interferes with ability to achieve desired goals
Experiences positive self-regard, which further promotes empathic responses	Often harbors resentments, since feelings are suppressed	Generates resentment in others due to abusive behavior	Harbors resentments and also generates them in others
Elicits trust and respect from others	Experiences self-denigration	Experiences frustration and questions value	Experiences decreasing self-esteem and a sense of helplessness
	Tendency to get even through passive-aggressive acts, reducing trust and respect in others	Destroys trust and respect in others	Destroys trust and respect in self and others

them to. The goal is to identify alternatives. If all I know how to do is curse or hit someone, my options are limited. Once alternatives are identified, I may choose another course of action, or I may still decide to curse or hit someone. MY response is always, "Keep an open mind and see if you can learn something new. You are still in charge of how you respond and can do whatever you want—as long as you are prepared to accept the consequences for your choices."

When introducing the exercise, the following instructions are given to reduce defensive reactions:

1. View current patterns of communication from a no-fault perspective. Individuals do the best they can with the skills at hand. If you are not aware that alternative response choices exist, is it realistic to approach negative outcomes with the thought, "If I only knew then what I know now?"

2. Avoid the tendency to compare yourself with others. We all have unique ways of feeling, thinking, and responding, and what is appropriate for one individual may not be for another.

3. The anger management-relapse prevention program strives to strengthen interpersonal relationships and sustain sobriety. The goal is *not* to use past experiences as opportunities to blame and shame ourselves or others. This is a learning experience, *not* a persecution!

4. Individuals have well-defined patterns for approaching conflict that are influenced by the following:

- *The nature of the conflict:* How significant the issue is in the greater scheme of things. The value we attach to an issue generating conflict directly influences the intensity of our reactions. Issues considered very important generate much stronger reactions than do those identified as negotiable.
- *The state of our relationship with the other party:* For nonaddicted individuals, conflict may be more intense if the relationship is perceived as secure (I may yell or disagree, and I know from past experience you will still love me). Conversely, recovering addicts and alcoholics may experience reduced conflict in significant relationships due to shame and guilt over past actions (I have no right to be angry/disagree). Personal styles must be carefully investigated to avoid explosive outbursts or

acquiescent responses that possess the potential to damage relationships and initiate relapse.

- *Demographics and related factors:* Age, health, legal status, financial situation, emotional state, and our perceptions regarding these factors all play a role in response choices involving conflict. The less stable I am, or perceive I am, the more likely I will be to assume a defensive posture. On the contrary, if I am secure, and perceive myself in this light, I am more likely to assume a nondefensive posture.
- *The anticipated outcome:* My perception of the potential consequences of an interaction or event will significantly influence my response choices. If I perceive the potential for a positive outcome, I will assume a cooperative, nondefended position. If, however, I perceive myself at risk for negative consequences, I may assume a defensive, guarded posture.
- *The* subjective *level of distress generated by the conflict:* It is critical to remember that what may seem inconsequential to one person may be unbearable to another. Again, perception plays a powerful role in response choices.

5. Each of these communication styles have applications in certain life circumstances; the labels good or bad do not apply. Although empathic responses are generally the most appropriate choice for day-to-day situations, aggressive responses are certainly appropriate when an individual is threatened with injury or death. Passive responses are also useful in the face of unpredictable reactions of psychotic, intoxicated, or enraged individuals. Even passive-explosive responses have practical application: If I am exposed to a situation where I am trapped, I may assume a passive demeanor while waiting for the appropriate opportunity to strike or flee. Since faulty perceptions can lead to unproductive response choices, a goal of this training program is to help you determine when to apply particular response choices.

6. Decisions to modify behavior are based on *perceived* benefits and costs of current responses. If I can continue to act out, threaten, and demand, or hold others hostage with passive or passive-explosive behavior, I have little motivation to change. If, however, my current response choices generate unpleasant consequences, I will be more inclined to evaluate and modify them.

Once these ground rules are established, Table 5 is reviewed, and clients are given opportunities to identify personal response styles and discuss how these patterns evolved. Sharing personal experiences helps participants understand that *everyone* has a point of view that *they* perceive as valid and true. This realization, although disquieting to some, can generate a sense of comfort. The perception that things can be defined as "different," not "right or wrong," reduces defensiveness, since different does not automatically mean "bad." Clients are invited to avoid falling prey to egocentric thinking (my way is the only right way), and instead to assume a position of curiosity: "I may not agree with you, but I am curious to hear your point of view and where it comes from."

Resistance predictably escalates at this point. Generally, I have activated someone's negative self-talk and receive a verbal attack. "Gee, Jo, are you saying it's OK for me to let my child run in front of a car? I *know* they shouldn't do it, but according to your theory, they should have the right to do what they want, regardless of the consequences." This presents an excellent opportunity to confront resistance and rationalization. My usual response is "Of course, certain situations, especially those involving individuals who are too young or emotionally incapacitated to make sound decisions, mandate an absolutist stand. It is not acceptable to murder an innocent person, to allow a child to dash into the street, to permit an elderly person with Alzheimer's to die from neglect. Just as we discovered there are justifiable applications of acquiescent, combative, and passive-explosive responses, there are times when an absolutist stance is essential. The trick is learning to identify faulty perceptions that evoke rigid, absolutist response choices in situations where they are not valid." This comment generally shuts down further resistance, and the session turns to a second task, applying alternative response choices to a series of preplanned situations in order to demonstrate that most situations offer more than one response choice (refer to Worksheet 6 and its accompanying answer sheet, pp. 176–179).

These defensive reactions are based on social norms. As children we learn that the "right" response is *always* one that preserves personal integrity and self-respect. Compromise, *for any reason*, is perceived as unacceptable. This philosophy severely limits response choices. Problem solving encourages clients to screen self-talk for biases discounting the reality that certain circumstances require alternative responses. Before group members can protest, the leader focuses on the example of robbery at gunpoint. Although short-term consequences include the loss of material possessions, the long-term benefit of self-preservation makes it judicious to deviate from traditional norms.

To further support this argument, the examples of someone cutting in line at the bank and the angry restaurant patron are revisited. Attempts to strong-arm a mentally unbalanced or inebriated person, or an extremely irate individual, increase the risk of violence. The sense of "being in control" quickly transforms into negative outcomes for participants and bystanders. Clients are reminded that they *always* have the right to choose their responses, but they must accept responsibility for the ensuing consequences. To conclude this very difficult session, clients are left to ponder the following thoughts:

1. Is being "right" so important that you are willing to die for it?
2. Have you damaged or ended relationships just to prove a point?
3. Are you in such a hurry that 5 minutes to consider options is never an option?
4. Is "saving face" more important than salvaging a situation?

Clients are instructed, "If you answered *yes* to any of the preceding questions, PLEASE consider *these* thoughts—they may save your life!"

1. Could more than one correct response exist?
2. Time is an ally—think before you act. It is easier not to act than to undo an act later.
3. There are times when courage means backing up, not charging ahead.
4. Words spoken quietly with conviction win more battles than those spoken in haste with anger.
5. Consider the other person's point of view *before* selecting your response. It may dramatically alter outcomes.
6. **Practice, practice, practice!** The only way to change existing responses is by practicing alternatives on a daily basis.

10

Asking for What You Want and Learning to Say No

Chapter 10 continues to explore the role negative feelings, self-defeating thoughts, poor self-esteem, and efficacy expectations play in perpetuating the anger-relapse cycle. Because response choices are the combined result of these variables, clients are reminded that unless interrupted, negative feelings and self-defeating thoughts will escalate into high-risk behaviors that culminate in relapse (Annis, 1986; Annis & Davis, 1987a, 1987b; Daley, 1988; Gorski & Miller, 1986; Marlatt & George, 1984; Marlatt & Gordon, 1985; Mueller & Ketcham, 1987; Potter-Efron & Potter-Efron, 1991a). The role interpersonal communication plays in active addiction and recovery makes it imperative to accomplish two tasks when developing strategies for relapse prevention. First, individuals must learn to recognize their thoughts, feelings, and needs, and the subtle shifts that occur when they are building up to relapse (see Chapters 3 and 4). Second, they must learn to effectively convey these thoughts, feelings, and needs to others (family members, friends, coworkers, and strangers we encounter in everyday situations) *before* selecting and activating response choices (see Chapters 7 and 9). Failure to accomplish these tasks significantly increases relapse potential.

An additional task essential to relapse prevention entails learning how to make and decline requests. Recovering addicts and alcoholics face several obstacles, particularly salient for this population, that further complicate this formidable task. First, the dysfunctional family rules "Don't talk, don't trust, don't feel" (Black & Buckey, 1986; Wegscheider, 1981; Wegscheider-Crus, 1976; Woititz, 1983) make it extremely difficult for these individuals to set limits and make requests. Past attempts to modify outcomes in this manner, while still enmeshed in dysfunctional relationships, were generally unsuccessful, and memories stemming from these experiences create deep-seated convictions that the open and direct expression of feelings and needs is a setup for disappointment. In essence, they learned how to displace or internalize thoughts and feelings and mask the emotional pain generated by unmet needs with alcohol and/or drug abuse. Reluctance to challenge this self-destructive pattern is reinforced by the second obstacle, self-defeating cognitions and the irrational beliefs and misperceptions that fuel them (Beck, 1987; DeRubeis & Beck, 1988; Ellis et al., 1988; Meichenbaum, 1986).

Historically, addicts and alcoholics pass through a series of losses as their addiction progresses. Absenteeism soon leads to unemployment, relationship conflicts end in divorce or estrangement, high-risk behaviors result in legal consequences, emotional distress, and declining health. Since this downward spiral is gradual, attempts to change occur only at crisis points and are quickly discarded once equilibrium is regained. These temporary states of sobriety become less and less frequent, and the chemically dependent individual feels more and more powerless to initiate change. Impoverished coping skills further exacerbate this dilemma, generating a pattern of self-defeating cognitions that immobilize the individual and obstruct pathways to recovery. Because our perceptions become our reality, the belief that change is impossible creates a self-fulfilling prophecy.

The third obstacle involves poor self-esteem arising from the shame and self-blame that characterize addiction (Potter-Efron & Potter-Efron, 1989). Active addiction creates incongruence in individuals' belief systems and response choices. Honesty, loyalty, and trust may be basic values; however, the need to obtain and use alcohol and drugs may lead to behaviors in direct conflict with these values (e.g., lying, stealing, cheating). Denial, rationalization, projection, and minimization create a trail of broken promises, miscommunications, and emotional pain that damage both interpersonal relationships and the core of one's self-esteem. The resulting shame and imploded anger create guilt and an urgent sense that penance must be paid. Unfortunately, the penance is never defined, and individuals fall into a pattern of self-denial and overextension. This inability to set limits and make requests fosters resentment (I shouldn't have to do this), which in turn exacerbates guilt (What am I thinking! After what I've done I have no right to complain), increasing the potential for relapse.

The fourth obstacle involves efficacy expectations (Daley, 1988). As discussed above, repeated failure to arrest the addictive process creates a pessimistic view of the potential for lasting change. Clients with chemical abuse and dependency diagnoses frequently adopt the belief that they are inept and cannot change (internalization of blame), rather than considering the possibility that they either do not possess adequate relapse prevention skills or neglected to apply their skills at critical points in the relapse process (external, situational approach; Marlatt & Gordon, 1985). Because efficacy expectations (the belief that I do/do not have the ability to change) directly influence outcome expectations (If I change, other things may/may not change, too), a negative perceptual set prevents individuals from setting limits and making requests. The belief that "no matter what I say or do things will never change" perpetuates the tendency to negate personal needs, overfunction in interpersonal relationships, and resort to alcohol and/or drug use to mask the emotional pain arising from unmet needs.

To remove or diminish these obstacles, recovering addicts and alcoholics must master the art of asking for what they want and need and of saying no when they feel overwhelmed or at risk of relapse. Teaching these skills is the primary focus of Session 9. This session emphasizes the fact that making and declining requests are two forms of interaction repeatedly encountered throughout an individual's life cycle. Most people cringe when confronted with the need to say no or to ask for something they need. An array of conflicting thoughts occur as we search for the "right" response. Two of the simplest words in the English language become notable relapse triggers when applied to recovering alcoholics and addicts. Although nonaddicted individuals also experience difficulty making and declining requests, the problem is magnified for those in recovery by the obstacles identified above. Reluctance to set limits and identify feelings and needs results in issue avoidance. The ensuing frustration provides a convenient excuse for relapse.

To reduce the stigma most clients in recovery feel regarding their inability to effectively set limits and communicate feelings and needs, the first task of this session involves reviewing six factors that have the potential to interfere with communication in *all* relationships:

1. *We fear rejection.* If we ask for something, we might not get it; therefore, we refrain from asking by rationalizing that we are unworthy of the other person's time and efforts. If a request is refused by us, we fear the person we turned down may shun us, therefore we may elect to help the person we wanted to say no to to avoid confrontation or rejection.

2. *The issue of commitment.* If we say yes, or no, how will this influence future interactions in the relationship? Will there be retaliation if we say no? Will the other person take advantage of us later if we accept help now?

3. *We adopt black-and-white thinking.* We overlook the fact that *everyone* offers help, at times, and always has the right to decline. The philosophy "all or nothing" exists in the distorted reality created by irrational thoughts. It is invalid in the rational world, where alternatives exist for those willing to investigate the points lying between these two extremes.

4. *We feel a need to provide an immediate response.* We fail to realize that asking for time to think is an acceptable alternative. As long as a response is provided within an identified and reasonable length of time, the need to evaluate current commitments before deciding whether an additional request can be honored is a rational approach to avoiding emotional overload.

5. *We believe a justifiable answer must always exist.* Only in the event of a *dire* emergency should help be solicited or requests refused, we believe, and even then we feel obligated to provide justifiable explanations. Although we may choose to provide an explanation, this is not essential and need not be lengthy or involved. Indeed, most people prefer a simple yes or no answer with a brief justification.

6. *We are afraid others will label us.* We place undue emphasis on what others think when we say no or ask for help. Self-defeating cognitions play a primary role in this process. We project our own thoughts onto others, often with gross inaccuracy, and fabricate the worst possible outcomes: "They'll think I don't care, that I'm lazy, that I'm just in it for what I can get" or "They'll think I'm a pushover, that I'm easy, that I can be had for a song."

The reality that *all* relationships experience the presence of these factors in varying degrees erodes the myth that only addicted family systems experience disruptions in communication. This intervention dilutes the rationalization "If only I wasn't an addict/alcoholic this relationship would be perfect" and places responsibility for need fulfillment on the individual. It also elicits resistance and skepticism, especially from clients with high denial, that expressing feelings and needs can influence outcomes. A frequent response is "Hey, Jo, that may be true, but what about the four obstacles we experience that other people generally don't have to face? We are *really* set up for failure." An analogy is used to challenge this self-defeating cognition.

There once was a great thoroughbred racehorse named Man o' War. This horse was so magnificent he outran every horse matched against him and finished races many furlongs ahead of the second fastest horse. In an attempt to even the odds, race officials required Man o' War's owner to add 30 pounds of lead weight to his saddle pads to handicap his speed. Since races were both long and arduous, this created a great hardship for Man o' War. Despite these odds, this magnificent horse continued to win most of his races. After telling this story, I invite clients to realize that each of us carries handicaps in one form or another. The challenge is to avoid becoming obsessed with our handicaps, so our energies can be redirected toward identifying and mobilizing our strengths. A review of the benefits and costs of setting limits and sharing versus withholding feelings and needs provides clients with a visible means to further evaluate this concept (see Table 6).

Clients are genuinely surprised to learn that failing to set limits and identify feelings makes them responsible for their unmet needs. Although we cannot control the responses of others, modifying *our* responses can significantly influence outcomes. Clearly stating preferences and dislikes is the first step in this process. The honest expression of feelings does not guarantee that others will satisfy our needs or respond graciously when we decline requests; however, it can reduce the potential for miscommunication.

Since conflict is inevitable, at times, despite our best intentions, what then is the value of honest communication? Clearly defining boundaries, informing others of wants and needs, and providing opportunities for problem solving gives rise to cooperative efforts. This reciprocity affords each individual a position of power and equality. Successful

Table 6
Sharing versus Withholding Feelings and Needs

Benefits of Expressing Feelings and Needs	Costs of Avoiding the Expression of Feelings and Needs
1. Asking for what you want or need lets the other person know exactly what you are feeling, so he or she can avoid second-guessing your reactions and feel more comfortable giving an honest response.	**1.** Resentments based on the assumption that others *should know* how we feel fester and damage relationships.
2. If you say no rather than hedging, it lets the other person know you cannot meet his or her needs, freeing the person to explore other options instead of hoping you'll come through.	**2.** We feel deprived or used. The other person is accused of insensitive behavior, despite the fact that he or she never had an opportunity to hear and respond to our feelings or needs.
3. Saying no when you mean no will allow you to avoid feeling trapped. This will reduce resentments and the potential for conflict with the requester at a later time.	**3.** We become hostile and demanding or play passive-aggressive games in an attempt to make the other person see the error of his or her ways. We irrationally assume the person *knows* what we *really* feel and are angered if he or she doesn't.
4. Stating true feelings is risky, but taking this risk can significantly reduce your relapse potential and create trust and mutually rewarding interactions with those you love.	**4.** Relapse occurs. If we can't get the recognition desired without asking or feel forced to perform tasks when we'd rather not, substance abuse may be used to punish others for not predicting our true feelings.
5. Defying the assumption that others should know how you feel will reduce tension and allow more realistic expectations to surface. This encourages future honesty and promotes integrity in relationships.	**5.** The assumption that others should know how we feel creates tension, since they inevitably fail to live up to our unrealistic expectations. This causes us to guard feelings even more closely and further estranges the actors in this perverse drama.

application of this approach involves helping clients understand how destructive self-talk can derail even their best efforts to set limits and make requests. To demonstrate this technique, the group leader shares several personal experiences. This self-disclosure reduces resistance and prepares clients for a subsequent group exercise.

LEADER EXAMPLE: ASKING FOR WHAT YOU NEED

In November, 1992, I experienced the near death of my infant son, born 13 weeks prematurely. After 4 months in the hospital, his discharge date arrived. Although I had accumulated 10 weeks of paid leave, additional time was needed to provide for his special needs. The competing interests of caring for my baby and preserving the family's financial integrity created a difficult dilemma.

Although self-talk messages dictated self-reliance at all costs, reality and exhaustion provided the incentive for me to practice my own techniques! Many colleagues offered to help but did not know what action to take. Several recommended the leave-transfer program. This special program allows employees to transfer vacation time to individuals with emergency situations. Challenging the messages "You don't deserve it! People won't give up their vacation time for you," I requested donations. The response provided income for my entire 6-month leave of absence!

Asking for assistance required me to confront several factors that interfere with the communication process:

1. Fear of rejection (People might say no.)
2. Self-esteem issues (I don't deserve such generosity.)
3. The issue of commitment (What paybacks will be expected?)

Allowing oneself to be vulnerable is the greatest challenge when applying this intervention. Although in this case the best possible outcome was realized, we do not always get what we want. Despite this reality, the greatest tragedy in relationships is failing to ask for help when it is needed. This deprives the potential recipient *and* potential donors of opportunities to give and receive help. Even when requests are denied, positive outcomes can materialize. Unfavorable responses motivate the requester to identify alternative solutions and prevent the receiver from accepting unwanted responsibility.

LEADER EXAMPLE: LEARNING HOW TO SAY NO

In the mid-1980s I was dating a man with an 8-year-old son. My own son was 9 years old. One day my boyfriend asked me to take both children to a Boy Scout function approximately 1 hour away. Although not really wanting to undertake this venture, I was determined to please my boyfriend, so I reluctantly said yes. The next day, two of my boyfriend's neighbors walked up to me and stated "We heard you offered to take our sons on the scouting trip, too—that's SO nice of you!" Feeling panic, I suppressed my true reaction. All the while, I fumed inside, telling myself, "What a dope you are! You don't know any of the people, have no idea where you're going, and will be stuck with five young boys in a small car for hours! How could he have volunteered my services without even asking?"

On the appointed day, I arrived to pick up the children. I followed another scouting parent on our route, hoping not to lose him, since I had no idea where we were going. After a grueling day I delivered the boys to their respective homes. Everyone thought I was a hero, having no idea how angry I was about the entire experience. A subsequent fight with my boyfriend confused him, since my response was out of proportion to the issue. Had I simply said no when the initial request was made, all this stress and frustration could have been avoided!

Soon thereafter, I developed the anger management-relapse prevention program and began practicing my own techniques. Since saying no was especially hard, I put extra effort into honestly asserting myself when confronted with unwanted requests. The ultimate test came 4 years later, when I remarried and converted to Catholicism. My new priest, upon learning I was a therapist, asked me to provide free counseling sessions to parish members. Old self-talk messages arose: "If you say no, what will he think of you? What if you need something from the church later and they remember when YOU said no?" I remembered the terrible scouting incident and how it had affected my self-esteem, so I decided to decline. I told the priest I was unable to accommodate this request at the present time. I was pleased and amazed when no terrible consequences came to pass. The honest expression of feeling allowed me to avoid feeling trapped and resentful. I later contributed 4 hours a month chaperoning church-sponsored junior high dances. Since this activity was self-selected, it allowed me to support the church *and* control the allocation of my time.

These self-disclosures provide opportunities to model alternative behavior and demonstrate that even trained professionals find it difficult to disclose feelings that may displease others. As further incentive, clients are encouraged to ask themselves two questions when responding to requests:

1. Will my response lead to the end of the world?
2. Will anyone die as a consequence of my response?

Although our decisions can create temporary imbalances in relationships, they rarely result in life-or-death consequences. A willingness to honestly express feelings eliminates the more realistic consequence—having to live through multiple unwanted experiences and the frustrations they create.

GROUP ACTIVITIES

Once clients digest this information, they complete an exercise in request management (see Worksheet 7, pp. 180–181). Participation in role plays and group discussion allows clients to practice making and declining requests, thereby preparing them for real-life interactions. Although client anxiety is high, the earlier therapist self-disclosure paves the way for client cooperation.

A review of the following guidelines for effective request management concludes this session (also see the client handout for Session 9):

1. We are accountable for our own responses, for initiating requests, and for establishing limits with others regarding what we can and cannot accomplish without jeopardizing sobriety.
2. Failure to express feelings honestly contributes to interpersonal conflict, miscommunications, and relapse.
3. The biggest hazard in life is inaction. Refusing to courageously state our convictions dooms us to an unfulfilled existence.
4. Life is a series of choices, not a narrow script of absolutes.
5. Taking risks creates avenues to success more often than pathways to defeat.

Therapists introducing this technique are often confronted with client resistance and skepticism for reasons identified earlier in this chapter. Although leader examples identify the dynamics that influence making and declining requests, a missing piece is the opportunity to review actual case studies. Therefore, two case examples will illustrate this intervention in action for clinicians reading this book.

CASE STUDY: MR. W.

Mr. W. is a middle-aged, married father of three. His alcohol dependence spans 25 years, and he explained multiple failed treatment attempts by stating, "I can stop for awhile, then my frustration gets the best of me and I start drinking again." While completing his social work assessment, I discovered a pattern of passive acquiescence. This client literally refused to openly express his feelings and needs to family members and silently seethed since his own needs were, in his opinion, repeatedly discounted. Following a 2- to 3-week buildup of negative feelings, self-defeating thoughts, and self-flagellation, he ultimately resorted to alcohol use, blaming family members for these relapse episodes: "If my family were more sensitive to my needs, this would stop happening!" The final straw occurred when his wife loaned a substantial amount of money to one of their adult daughters without first consulting him. His reaction was to implode anger and initiate a 2-week drinking binge. When he presented for treatment, he was facing a DWI charge, had alienated family members by withdrawing and refusing to discuss the issue, and expressed a sense of hopelessness and defeat.

Intervention

Mr. W. spent 10 days on a detoxification unit and was then transferred to an outpatient program. Since his wife and children agreed to participate in treatment, he was concurrently enrolled in the anger management-relapse prevention training program and multifamily group. In anger management-relapse prevention training classes Mr. W. explored the influence of past experiences on his current response choices. He discovered a lifelong pattern of imploding feelings and resorting to alcohol use to diminish the emotional pain of repeated disappointments. This passive approach to conflict resolution served as a catalyst for learned helplessness and reinforced the self-defeating cognition "No matter what I say, things will never change." This in turn generated low self-esteem and pessimistic efficacy expectations, resulting in a self-fulfilling prophecy. After identifying this pattern, Mr. W. was guided through a series of exercises (time-out, detouring self-talk, problem solving, and request management) and provided with opportunities to practice application of these techniques during role-play exercises.

Once he felt comfortable applying these techniques in his anger management-relapse prevention group, he was encouraged to practice applying them to small issues with his family in multifamily group. He was initially highly resistant, stating, "It may work in anger management-relapse prevention group, but it will never work with my family." After further exploration of his resistance, he identified fear of rejection and black-and-white thinking as factors that interfered with his ability (willingness) to openly express feelings and needs. He was encouraged to challenge these factors and was reminded that his current response choices served only to further erode family cohesiveness. He reluctantly agreed and began to slowly identify his feelings to family members. They were genuinely shocked when he expressed his sense of hopelessness and indicated that he felt left out and discounted by other family members. He was equally surprised when they expressed their own sense of frustration and hopelessness, since repeated attempts to include him in family decisions were met with resistance and withdrawal. This family was assisted in developing a new pattern of communication that involved focusing on problems rather than on who is right or wrong, learning to negotiate and compromise when opposing needs created conflict, and identifying feelings and needs *before* frustration escalated to the point of relapse or withdrawal for the client and unilateral decision making by other family members.

Outcome

Contact with Mr. W. 1 year following treatment revealed improvement in his ability to set limits and identify feelings and needs. Although the family experienced periodic bouts of conflict, as does every family, Mr. W. had learned not to hold other family members hostage with withdrawal and threats of relapse. His family members had also expanded efforts to include him in making family decisions and reported less anxiety regarding their need to monitor responses to avoid triggering relapse episodes. Mr. W.'s sobriety was intact, and he continued to attend

Alcoholics Anonymous meetings in conjunction with the application of anger management-relapse prevention techniques. The family appeared more cohesive, and power struggles were significantly less evident than when the family initially presented for treatment.

CASE STUDY: MS. H.

Ms. H. is a 40-year-old, twice-divorced mother of two. She presented for treatment reporting a tremendous desire to arrest a 20-year history of alcohol and drug abuse. This client's pattern of alcohol and cocaine abuse created a series of negative consequences: two arrests on drug-related charges, chronic unemployment, estrangement from her two adult children, social isolation, and a fatalistic outlook on the potential for change. The precipitating factor that led her to seek treatment was termination from her most recent job and the threat of eviction from her apartment.

Intervention

Because this client's social stressors were severe, she was placed on an inpatient unit for detoxification and guidance in resolving immediate social needs (finance, housing, unemployment). She was assisted in applying for financial aid, referred for vocational and employment evaluation and placement, and encouraged to move into a recovery-oriented halfway house upon discharge to reduce her tendency to isolate herself and resort to alcohol and drug use. Following detoxification and resolution of her social stressors, she was enrolled in an outpatient program and placed in anger management-relapse prevention training.

Ms. H. identified a lifelong pattern of self-reliance stemming from her childhood. At age seven she was abandoned by her parents and placed in a series of foster homes. She experienced multiple episodes of physical and sexual abuse and learned to trust no one, relying only on her own ingenuity to survive until adulthood provided escape. Although this approach helped her survive childhood trauma, it generated the unrealistic belief that she could handle anything life might throw her way. Her extreme fear of abandonment, coupled with poor self-esteem and deficiencies in interpersonal skills, led to social avoidance and resistance to seek help until the situations in her life became so unbearable she could no longer go on.

The first intervention with Ms. H. involved challenging this self-defeating belief system. I invited her to practice requesting assistance, and her response was "I don't need any help, I can do it myself!" Even confrontation from several group members regarding past failures that were the direct result of trying to manage everything on her own were met with resistance and the rationalization that "if people would just leave me alone I could manage just fine!" Several analogies were used to help her identify the destructive consequences of her refusal to accept help. I first asked her to envision herself caught in quicksand. She was slowly sinking to her death and could not reach anything to pull herself out. A stranger suddenly appears and extends his hand, offering her an opportunity to survive. She was asked whether she would accept help under such extreme conditions. Her response was "I'm sure my rescuer would want something in return, so I might as well just die."

Since her attitude was severely fatalistic, a second, less threatening analogy was interjected. I asked her to envision an unkempt, stray dog that had been beaten and abused. This animal was near starvation and desperate for food. Despite this desperation, when a plate of food was placed on the ground several feet from the stranger attempting to help, the dog was so fearful it refused to eat. Unless the animal was courageous enough to overcome its extreme fear of the possibility of additional abuse at the hands of its potential rescuer, the outcome would be further suffering, and eventually death. Ms. H. was invited to see how her own situation could result in similar grim results unless she initiated action to interrupt her downward spiral. Since self-reliance was a predominant theme in her cognitions, emphasis was placed on the fact that it requires great courage to move beyond ourselves to accept help. She was also reminded that help can be accepted in degrees, and the person accepting help always has the right to terminate this process at any point if his or her anxiety becomes too great. She was encouraged to experiment with asking for and accepting help through role-play exercises in group.

Ms. H. reluctantly agreed. However, she maintained a pessimistic attitude. She was instructed to approach each group member and request a hug since she had identified a need to feel loved and accepted. Although this generated acute discomfort, she accomplished this task and received a positive response from all members. The group then assisted her in processing her thoughts and reactions to this experience. She was given homework assignments to practice asking for help with small issues to reduce anxiety and enhance skills application. An additional recommendation involved combining detouring self-talk with request management so she could monitor self-defeating cognitions that interfered with her ability to make requests and accept assistance.

Outcome

Ms. H. prematurely withdrew from treatment and has resurfaced several times since her initial admission. She continues to uphold her belief that no matter what she does, things will never change. Her prognosis, at present, is poor but not hopeless. Maintaining my own belief that change is always possible, my hope for Ms. H. is that eventually the combination of negative experiences and exposure to treatment will generate sufficient motivation to initiate change. Rather than viewing Ms. H. as a treatment failure, I prefer to adopt the attitude that she is not yet ready for change. My parting remarks to her during her last admission were "I know you may not be ready to follow my recommendations, but please remember that when your pain exceeds your fear, you will come to the realization that the only way out is through, and you will take action to alter your behavior. I wish you luck and hope you will keep me posted on how you are doing. Remember, I'm waiting in the wings to help if and when you decide you are ready."

11

Stress and the Anger-Relapse Cycle

By this point in treatment clients can identify many of the triggers and cues that fuel the anger-relapse cycle and have developed skills to interrupt this process. There is, however, an additional variable that significantly influences relapse potential: stress. Gorski and Miller (1986) identify stress as a natural byproduct of the recovery process. According to the developmental model of recovery (Gorski & Miller, 1986), individuals move through a variety of stages as they initiate, achieve, and maintain sobriety. Since recovery is a process and not an end state, numerous transitions, each generating specific stress reactions, occur as individuals pass through these stages. The changes encountered during this process activate what Selye (1956, 1974) described as a general adaptation syndrome. When the body encounters stress it reacts with alarm, activating a fight-or-flight mechanism. Successful resolution of stress results in an optimal biological adaptation (the body normalizes and returns to its prestress state). If, however, stress is unremitting, the body eventually reaches a state of exhaustion and disintegration, resulting in illness or death.

When this concept is applied to recovering alcoholics and addicts, an additional outcome stemming from chronic stress is relapse. Gorski and Miller (1986) refer to the phenomenon correlated with chronic stress as post-acute withdrawal (PAW): the physiological, psychological, and social reactions to abstinence from drugs and alcohol. PAW arises from the body's need to repair itself following a course of active addiction. Symptoms of this phenomenon occur in varying degrees for months after abstinence is achieved, as the stresses of recovery are encountered. Individuals experiencing PAW are particularly sensitive to stress and may have difficulty distinguishing between low- and high-level stress situations. Cognitive distortions regarding self-efficacy, outcome expectancy, and the attributes of causality further complicate this process (Daley, 1988; Marlatt & Gordon, 1985). The interaction of PAW and negative cognitions activates a destructive chain reaction that begins with frustration and quickly escalates to exhaustion and despair. The resulting physical and mental distress adversely affects the body's ability to cope with stress and, if not interrupted, culminates in relapse.

Because stress plays a critical role in the anger-relapse cycle, Sessions 10 and 11 are devoted to stress management. Beginning in Session 10 with a basic review of stress as it applies to all individuals, the leader depicts stress as a phenomenon that exists along a continuum ranging from not enough stress at one end to stress overload at the other. Identifying stress as a dynamic, ever-present aspect of life short-circuits the belief that all stress is bad and should be avoided. To facilitate this process, clients are asked to answer two questions: (1) What is stress? and (2) Is all stress bad? Responses to these questions serve two purposes: (1) They allow the leader to evaluate clients' current beliefs about stress, and (2) they provide opportunities to replace misconceptions with fact.

When clients define stress, they generally focus on unpleasant or destructive side-effects: upset stomachs, headaches, anxiety, relapse, and depression. Positive aspects, such as incentives to develop and pursue goals and the motivation to achieve one's potential, are frequently overlooked. This biased perspective impedes recovery by providing clients with a convenient excuse to avoid *all* stress (e.g., attending group therapy or Alcoholics Anonymous meetings). Reality testing challenges this irrational thinking (see Table 7).

The inevitable question clients pose after reviewing Table 7 is "That's all well and good, Jo, but how do we know when stress is healthy and when it's destructive?" The following guidelines help answer this question: Healthy stress produces enough tension to generate movement toward goals but not so much that we feel overwhelmed. Distress arises

Table 7
Healthy Stress versus Distress

MYTH: All stress is bad and should be avoided.
REALITY: Stress responses, depending on the circumstances, have the potential to create positive *and* negative consequences.

Healthy Stress	Distress
Stimulates thinking	Inhibits thinking
Motivates change	Discourages change
Promotes productive risk taking	Interferes with risk taking
Provides a mechanism for self-preservation	Diminishes personal power
Enhances personal growth	Creates reactive behavior
Generates new ideas	Impairs personal growth
Maintains interest in living	Interferes with idea formation
Enhances mood	Leads to apathy
Increases self-esteem	Depresses mood
Creates opportunities	Damages self-esteem
Raises energy level	Blocks opportunities
Contributes to high productivity	Reduces energy level
Creates a sense of contentment	Creates a pressured, intense mood
Helps create a balanced lifestyle	Leads to disorganization and despair

when high levels of stress, not readily amenable to change, bombard us. Because individual responses to stress are highly variable, what feels comfortable to one person may send another into overload. An analogy helps illustrate this distinction.

Imagine a dog that has been raised by a sedate, elderly couple. This animal is accustomed to living indoors, receiving his meals at predictable times each day, having regular outings for relief, and going on a daily walk. The dog receives regular attention from his masters; however, he rarely sees outsiders since the couple rarely goes out or entertains company. In this setting, the dog is exposed to enough stress to elicit contentment (pleasant responses from his masters, daily walks, a comfortable pillow to sleep on, adequate food, and regular trips outside to relieve himself) but not so much stress that he feels threatened or uncomfortable.

Imagine this same dog 10 years later, now much older and definitely set in his ways. His owners, elderly 10 years ago, predictably deteriorate and die. The dog suddenly finds himself living with his masters' adult daughter, her husband, and three rambunctious sons. Although well cared for, the dog experiences many changes: He is relocated to a doghouse in the backyard, fed at unpredictable times each day as someone remembers to set out a dish of food, and walked infrequently. The amount of activity in his environment increases dramatically as family members and a host of friends and relatives come and go in a fashion as unpredictable as mealtime and walks. The dog, once living with a productive level of stress, finds himself overwhelmed and disoriented. The resulting distress generates changes in his mood (irritability, avoidance), appetite (picky eating and weight loss), and daily habits (when and where he eliminates, sleeps, exercises). Unless the dog can adjust to this traumatic lifestyle change, he may become ill and die.

Let's reverse the story and describe a second dog raised in an active, highly stimulating environment. This dog lives outside and has learned that his masters will feed and walk him daily, but also knows there is no predictable pattern for these activities. He is accustomed to roughhousing with children and regular visits from a variety of neighbors, family members, and friends, and seldom experiences boredom since someone is always petting or talking to him. Then one of the adults in the family receives a promotion that necessitates a move overseas, and the dog must be left behind. The family pleads with Grandma, a widow living alone, to keep the dog while they are gone. The dog moves to a quiet, highly regimented setting. He lives inside and is fed and walked at predictable times; although Grandma treats him kindly, she continues her daily routine much the same as before the dog came. She rarely goes out or has company, so the dog receives little stimulation. This dramatic decrease in stimulation creates distress that results in changes in mood (avoidance or excessive attempts to gain attention), appetite (weight gain due to boredom and overeating, or weight loss due to depression), and daily habits. This dog must also make adjustments necessary to accommodate his lifestyle change or face the same fate as did the dog described in the first scenario.

The purpose of these analogies is to help clients understand that change, in any direction, creates at least a temporary state of distress. Whether distress is successfully navigated and defused hinges on two factors: the presence of adequate coping skills, and a willingness to be flexible and make adjustments as the process unfolds. A third analogy is used to emphasize the importance of flexibility. Clients are first asked to picture a redwood tree. This huge, stately tree is at least a century old, stands 50 feet high, and is as big around as a tanker truck. Next, they are asked to picture a willow tree. Small and supple, bending and swaying with the wind, this tree is dwarfed by its neighbor, the redwood. Finally, they are asked to envision a tremendous hurricane with high winds, fierce rain, and hail. The redwood and the willow, exposed to the full force of this storm, struggle for existence. After the storm, a survey of the damage reveals startling results: The redwood tree, unable to bend and sway with the wind, was uprooted and killed. Surprisingly, the tiny willow, although bent and tattered, is still standing. Its flexibility allowed it to bend and sway with the storm. This tree will recover and go on to weather future storms.

When applying this concept to recovery, clients are cautioned that stress must be sufficient to motivate active participation in treatment, but not so great that it triggers relapse. Referring to Gorski and Miller's (1986) explanation of PAW, clients are given a description of the developmental model of recovery. A series of stressors, referred to as motivational crises, are encountered during this process, especially as individuals make transitions from one stage to the next. Flexibility, both cognitive and behavioral, is essential to navigate the array of "stuck points" experienced along the way. Confronted with anger, denial, rationalization, depression, and a host of other self-defeating reactions, recovering addicts and alcoholics must creatively apply techniques to dissolve these "stuck points." Because inflexibility frequently masquerades in the guise of negative feelings, self-defeating thoughts, and poor self-esteem, the key to regaining equilibrium following an episode of distress involves identifying stress warning signs and taking immediate action to arrest their progression. Failure to acknowledge and heed these warnings exacerbates "stuck points," derailing the recovery process.

Since most clients have limited knowledge regarding stress and its variable presentations, they frequently find themselves in stress overload with no idea of how they got there. A former client, exasperated by my insistence that stress warning signs can be identified and arrested, stated, "Jo! I don't go through those subtle changes in my feelings, body reactions, thoughts, and behavior that you keep describing. I find myself feeling fine one minute and then, suddenly, I'm thrust into overload." My response was "I have never met a person who could go from 0 to 60 mph in 5.2 seconds. You are not a Ferrari, you are a human being! You may not be *aware* of these subtle changes, but they *do* exist." Next, I challenged this client to use his anger journal to heighten his awareness of triggers and cues. He was reminded that awareness is the first step to the successful interruption of this process. A review of the physical, cognitive, emotional, and behavioral cues identified in Session 3 (Chapter 4), and identification of four additional factors influencing the anger-relapse cycle, is helpful at this point during the session.

The correlation between excessive stress and relapse make it essential to review these factors, despite their previous introduction in Session 3. Clients (and the rest of us, too!) rarely grasp concepts on the first pass. This reinforcement empowers clients to recognize and counteract potential relapse triggers. Rapid, well-planned interventions are critical, since they can mean the difference between sobriety and relapse. Principal warning signs include the following:

- **Physical complaints**, such as headaches, backaches, ulcers, high blood pressure, and other physical discomforts
- **Changes in behavior**, including changes in eating or sleep patterns, decreased productivity at work or school, poor personal hygiene, or withdrawal from activities or friends
- **Changes in emotional states**, manifested as depression, fatigue, increased irritability, anxiety, distractibility, or simply feeling overwhelmed by daily routines
- **Shifts in cognitions**, such as rationalizations that recreational alcohol/drug use is still possible, making negative comments about attending recovery-related activities, or frequenting high-risk situations (bars, parties, visiting drinking/using associates)

Following a discussion of these warning signs, four additional variables that significantly influence recovery are identified.

1. *The nature of the stressor* (short-term, chronic, or combined). Intensity and duration are critical determinants in this process. The more severe the stressor, and the longer its duration, the greater the potential for stress overload. The symbolic meaning of the stressor also influences this factor. The more value placed on a particular stressor and its potential outcome, the greater its impact on an individual's ability to effectively mobilize the resources necessary for successful resolution.
2. *Perceptions regarding ability to resolve the stressors.* Efficacy expectations (Daley, 1988) significantly influence response choices. If I believe my actions will have no effect, I am likely to passively accept the consequences arising from a particular stressor. If, however, I believe I can initiate action to redirect the outcome, my response is more likely to be assertive.
3. *Personal tolerance levels for stress.* Personality characteristics, past experiences, existing supports, and availability of coping skills all interact to influence this variable. The greater my resilience and ability to identify and mobilize resources for stress reduction, the more likely I am to achieve a positive outcome.
4. *The presence or absence of adequate coping skills to resolve stressors.* If I possess a well-rounded repertoire of coping skills, I am more likely to manage stress effectively. Poorly defined or absent coping skills contribute to the escalation of stress, increasing relapse potential.

Following this review of triggers and cues, a description of short-term, chronic, and combined stress reactions is provided (see Figures 4, 5, and 6). This comparison highlights variable reactions produced by stress and provides a baseline for recognizing when stress overload is imminent. The models are drawn on the board to visually display similarities and differences, and clients are invited to place themselves in the model that best describes their current stress level. The fact that we each have highly variable stress adaptability limits is reemphasized to reduce the risk of comparison and minimization (my problem isn't really that bad if you compare it to X.'s). This is followed by a discussion of each model.

Short-term stress, depicted in Figure 4, is described as a *temporary disruption* that occurs when movement toward a specific goal is derailed or blocked. The stressor is generally mild or moderate in nature and seldom has far-reaching consequences. This type of stress is adaptive because it prompts us to mobilize and direct our energies into resolving the problem. An individual experiencing short-term stress *temporarily* feels off-balance, but quickly regains control by taking action to eliminate sources of distress. Examples include spilling a glass of milk, having a flat tire, or forgetting to bring your résumé to a job interview. In the first example, corrective action might be cleaning up the spill and pouring another glass of milk. In the second, calling for road service or changing the flat yourself handles the matter. In the final example, explaining your mistake and mailing a résumé resolves the dilemma.

Resolution of short-term stress is accomplished quickly, freeing the individual to redirect energies elsewhere. Within a matter of hours, incidents are forgotten or become anecdotes shared with others to discharge residual frustration. Unless multiple short-term stressors occur simultaneously or are superimposed on chronic stressors, they generate minimal discomfort and can stimulate us to engage problem-solving skills.

Clients can easily identify short-term stress since it abounds in daily transactions. Typical examples include traffic jams; long or slow lines in banks, supermarkets, or other businesses; arguments with significant others; or misplacing eyeglasses, a favorite book, or car keys. Although easily identified, most clients never consider the impact short-term stressors have on recovery. A primary objective of this session is to help clients develop awareness of and control over short-term stress so it becomes a source of motivation for rather than an impediment to recovery.

Chronic stress, depicted in Figure 5, is much more dramatic than short-term stress, both in intensity and duration. This type of stress can take one of two paths: an unexpected stressor occurs, placing the individual in a state of massive change (sudden death of a loved one; unanticipated divorce), or a series of stressors produces negative results across time (disfiguring accident; permanent disability; terminal illness). In each case, the individual has limited ability, at least initially, to mobilize resources necessary to minimize harmful consequences.

A disfiguring accident or permanent disability immediately affects self-image, relationships, and, possibly, mobility. Far-reaching consequences may include job loss, leading to financial crisis, which could

Figure 4. Model 4: Short-Term Stress Response

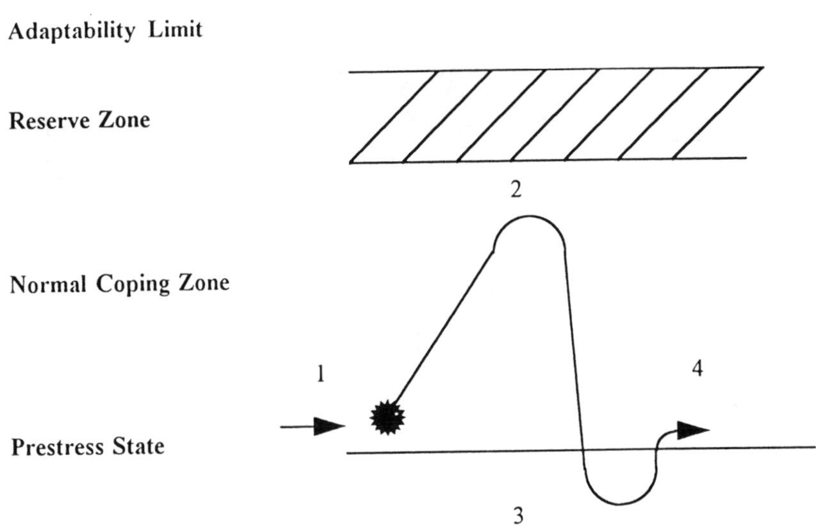

1. A stressful event occurs.
2. Coping responses are mobilized and stressors are resolved within the normal coping zone. The reserve zone, much like a savings account, is a resource for additional energy, but is not needed unless multiple stressors occur simultaneously.
3. The individual experiences a brief recovery period, during which body functions and emotions return to normal.
4. Equilibrium is regained and normal activities are resumed. No long-term effects are experienced, and energy reserves remain intact and available for future resolutions.

Adapted, with permission of the publisher, from: Munz, D. (1983). *Stress management participant's manual*. St. Louis: St. Louis University Medical Center—Healthline.

Figure 5. Model 5: Chronic Stress Response

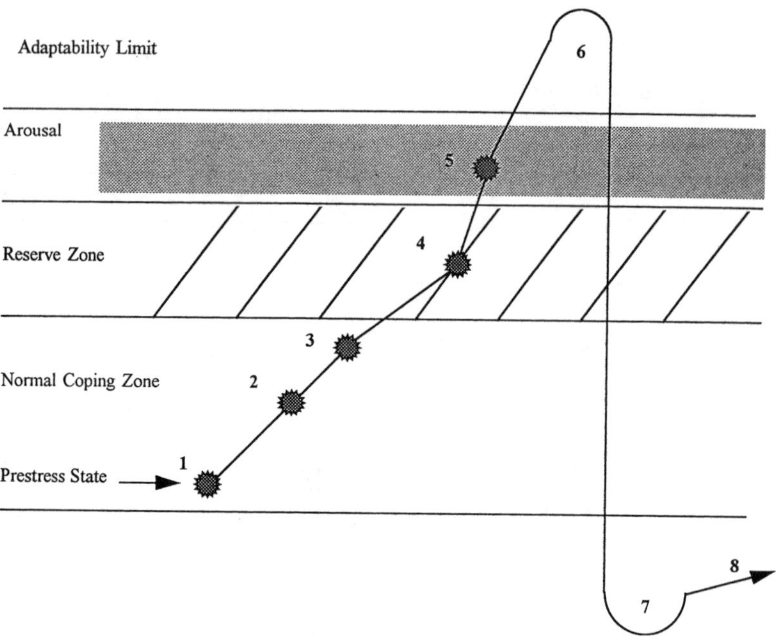

1. A stressful event occurs.
2. Coping responses are mobilized; however, more stress is added before the original stressor is resolved.

3-5. Stressors continue to mount as the individual attempts to regain control. Reserve energies are drawn upon and exhausted, forcing the individual to extend himself or herself beyond safe limits.

6. Stress overload occurs. There is no more energy to effectively cope, and the individual reaches a state of disorganization.
7. A delayed recovery period begins. The individual is highly susceptible to physical illness, emotional distress, burnout, and relapse.
8. The individual struggles to regain normal functioning and can be catapulted into overload by the slightest stressor.

Adapted, with permission of the publisher, from: Munz, D. (1983). *Stress management participant's manual*. St. Louis: St. Louis University Medical Center—Healthline.

threaten continuity of basic needs (housing, food, medical care). Although a series of interventions can help the individual adapt to these losses, it is a lengthy process, precluding instant stress reduction. Considerable trauma occurs before the situation begins to stabilize. Likewise, an unexpected death or divorce creates imbalance in the family system that escalates as the impact defuses to all facets of the individual's life. Again, interventions to address this situation exist; however, high levels of distress occur before relief becomes available.

Clients are less successful in identifying chronic stress since the addiction process distorts perceptions of reality. Chronic stress, a predictable side-effect of long-term substance abuse, is identified as the "cause," not the consequence of active addiction. Responsibility for generating a corrective response is magically negated. Clients fail to realize that continued substance use exacerbates rather than ameliorates chronic stress.

Helping clients assess stress configurations becomes significant when short-term stress is superimposed on chronic stress, creating a combined stress reaction (see Figure 6). Under these circumstances, a seemingly insignificant event generates extreme reactions. Individuals in recovery routinely face the double negative of combined stress reactions. Already struggling to change longstanding patterns of behavior, minor incidents quickly overwhelm them. The lack of support and encouragement characterizing addictive family systems, although predictable, further magnifies their sense of isolation and frustration. To contain this risk factor, clients are cautioned to avoid lifestyle changes not directly related to recovery *for at least 6 months*, whenever possible. The goal is to firmly establish sobriety *before* undertaking additional challenges.

An analogy is used to help clients understand the combined stress reaction and to encourage limit setting and realistic expectations regarding recovery (i.e., it will not happen overnight; there will be setbacks). Since I work in the Houston Veterans Affairs Medical Center, my caseload is predominantly male, which explains the following analogy. I ask clients to envision a brand-new pair of Jockey underwear. Next, I ask them, "What happens when you put it on, pull the elastic away from your body, and let go?" The inevitable response is "It snaps back, and it hurts like hell!" I then ask them to envision the same pair of Jockey underwear after 1000 washes in hot water with bleach. I again ask, "What happens

Figure 6. Model 6: Combined Stress Reaction

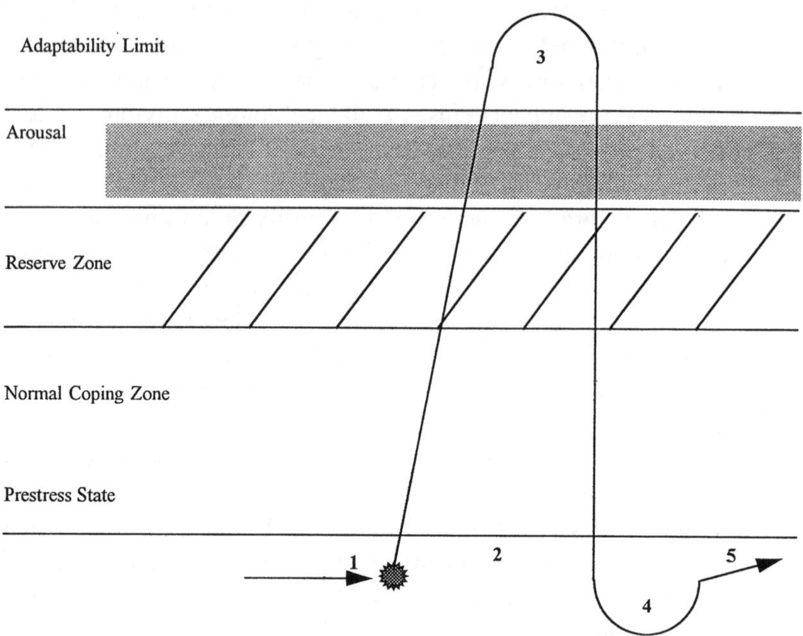

1. The individual is in a delayed state of recovery due to the chronic stressor(s) in his or her life.
2. A short-term stressor is encountered.
3. The individual immediately experiences stress overload and is unable to mobilize coping skills needed to resolve the stressor.
4. Once the crisis has passed, the individual plunges back into a delayed recovery period and remains at risk for further trauma due to his or her vulnerable condition.
5. Attempts to return to a prestress level of functioning are further impaired, creating a sense of helplessness and despair. Risk of relapse is extreme during this phase of the stress response.

Adapted, with permission of the publisher, from Munz, D. (1983). *Stress management participant's manual*. St. Louis: St. Louis University Medical Center—Healthline.

when you put it on, pull it away from your body, and let go?" The response this time is "The elastic is gone, and it falls down around my ankles!" Finally, I ask, "What do you do once the underwear wears out?" The usual response is "I buy a new pair."

Our psyches, much like Jockey underwear, have limited resilience. We can only subject ourselves to a certain amount of stress before our emotional elastic wears out. Since we can't throw out our mind and purchase a new one, the task becomes one of damage containment and restoration. This entails limiting the addition of new sources of stress, requesting assistance in managing or resolving the stress we currently carry and cannot unload, and allowing time to rebuild the emotional reserves necessary to cope with stress effectively.

A final directive before moving on to a discussion of strategies for stress management concerns the issue of positive stress. Although promotions and awards are signs of upward mobility, clients are cautioned that positive stress can precipitate relapse. This warning elicits resistance, so the story of Mr. Q., a former client who experienced relapse following 2 years of continuous sobriety, is shared. Mr. Q. received a promotion and a $10,000 raise. He failed to consider the impact this event might have on his sobriety. Added responsibilities interfered with his participation in recovery-related activities. This reduction of support coincided with increasing job-related pressures, setting the stage for relapse. He was successful in regaining sobriety and learned an important lesson: Positive stress must be carefully monitored to avoid stress overload and relapse.

12

Stress Management as a Relapse Prevention Tool

Once clients develop a basic awareness of stress reactions, contributing factors, and possible consequences, they are encouraged to play an active role in managing this aspect of recovery. Session 11 introduces skills necessary for them to accept and meet this challenge. The first task involves reviewing commonsense rules our parents taught us during childhood:

1. Eat a balanced diet.
2. Make sure you get an adequate amount of rest.
3. Exercise daily to foster a sense of well-being.
4. Develop a network of friends to share the good times and support you during times of trouble.

These directives form cornerstones for all stress management interventions. Without adequate nutrition, rest, exercise, and support, the effectiveness of any intervention, no matter how innovative, is greatly reduced. Revisiting an analogy presented in the previous session reinforces the importance of these directives. Clients are invited to remember the analogy introduced during Session 10 of new versus well-worn

Jockey underwear. When new, the elastic waistband in a pair of Jockey underwear snaps back snugly after being pulled out and released. The same pair of underwear after 1000 washes in hot water with bleach deteriorates rapidly. The once supple elastic no longer snaps back when pulled out and released—it falls down around your ankles!

The human body is very similar. If we take care of ourselves (good diet, rest, exercise, support), everyday frustrations resolve in the normal coping zone, leaving reserves available for times of exceptional stress. When neglected (poor diet, inadequate rest, no exercise, minimal or nonexistent supports), we quickly show signs of physical and emotional distress, dramatically increasing the risk of relapse. Therefore, the first step in stress management involves developing healthy lifestyle practices (Davis, 1984; Ketcham & Mueller, 1981; Milam & Ketcham, 1981). This is an especially difficult task for recovering alcoholics and addicts, whose bodies have suffered years of abuse and neglect. They frequently enter treatment in poor condition, lacking energy and skills needed to design a daily self-care plan. Since group time is limited, the leader initiates referrals to programs promoting recovery-oriented behavior.

Another important aspect of effective stress management involves assessing response choices. Although clients generally have well-established repertoires of behavior when stress is encountered, they often overlook repetitive patterns of defeat. The application of uncomfortably familiar coping styles (e.g., drinking, drug use, overeating, impulsive sex acts, overspending), driven in part by self-defeating thoughts, often lies beyond clients' perceptual awareness (Beck, 1976, 1987; Ellis 1962, 1971, 1973, 1985, 1988; Ellis & Bernard, 1985; Ellis & Dryden, 1987; Ellis & Greiger, 1977, 1986; Ellis & Harper, 1975; Ellis et al., 1988; Ellis & Whiteley, 1979; Meichenbaum, 1977, 1986). Failure to recognize this critical connection produces a self-perpetuating cycle of stress, reactivity, and relapse. Closer examination of the interplay between cognitions and subsequent response choices promotes identification and destruction of this cycle (see Worksheet 8, pp. 184–185).

Reviewing existing response choices helps clients recognize their mutual struggle to manage stress, appropriately redirect anger, and avoid relapse. Group members identify their personal responses, which are then reviewed collectively by the group. Inevitably, someone will challenge the assignment of specific variables to the categories "positive" and "negative." A typical comment is "Hey, Jo, you have sleep as an escape listed as a negative stress management strategy, but taking a short nap is listed as a positive stress management strategy. How can one be good and the other bad since they're related?" My response is "Whether a coping strategy is defined as positive or negative (not good or bad) is a function of intensity and duration. If I use books to escape and avoid social contact, then this coping strategy becomes a negative. But if I read 1 to 2 hours a day and continue to involve myself with other activities as well, it remains a positive coping strategy. The key to success is moderation."

At this point, one of my more oppositional clients generally chimes in with a comment like "Jo, does that mean suicide is a positive coping skill if I only kill myself a little?" To avoid this attempt at derailment, my typical response is "The goal of this exercise is to help you identify and eliminate negative coping strategies, and replace them with more productive alternatives." The leader provides several examples to demonstrate this process in action (see the following leader examples).

LEADER EXAMPLE: ANTICIPATING THE WORST OUTCOME

When confronted with a stressful event, you currently anticipate the worst possible outcome. Hours are wasted reviewing possibilities, and, of course, each one is even more horrible than the one preceding. These ruminations inevitably occur at night and lead to sleeplessness and despair. The next morning finds you bleary eyed, distraught, and totally unprepared to face the monster generating this mountain of distress. When the day of reckoning finally arrives, the outcome seldom produces the catastrophic results anticipated. You chastise yourself for being so ridiculous and vow *never* to let it happen again. Life returns to normal until the next stressor appears. You immediately forget your pledge, and, thus, the cycle continues.

A productive alternative is to *immediately* apply detouring self-talk. During this process, consciously remember your tendency to fabricate unpleasant results when facing the unknown. Consider that outcomes seldom develop as predicted, so it is unlikely this experience will deviate significantly from the norm. Redirect your activities to prevent rumination, and look for opportunities to approach a trusted friend or relative with whom to discuss the issue. Finally, actively apply the problem-solving model to minimize or eliminate the stressor.

LEADER EXAMPLE: AVOIDING SOCIAL CONTACT

When confronted with stressful events, you currently avoid social contact with others, blaming them for the deplorable state of your existence. Each time someone *attempts* to offer support, you create roadblocks that even your most courageous friends won't tackle. Predictably, this tactic leaves you feeling neglected and abused. Although a direct result of *your* actions, loved ones are criticized for their lack of concern. Meanwhile, the original source of stress has reached gargantuan proportions. This destructive pattern continues until a crisis brings you to your senses. In many cases, the crisis is a return to addictive behavior.

A productive alternative calls for an *honest* assessment of existing behaviors and their impact on your ability to effectively manage stress. Following this assessment, share concerns with *trusted* loved ones to prevent hard feelings and withdrawal of support. Next, redirect energies formerly used to blame others toward problem resolution. Finally, confiding in a nonjudgmental person, such as an AA sponsor, provides emotional relief until the stressor is resolved.

GROUP EXERCISE

These examples set the stage for a group exercise in replacing negative responses with productive alternatives. Following the introduction of leader examples, clients are invited to select one or two negative coping skills they identified on Worksheet 8. The remaining time for this portion of the session is devoted to practice applications and group feedback. A typical session generates responses similar to those presented below:

1. *Current Response:* Using sleep as an escape.
   Alternative Response: Take a *short* (30-minute) nap followed by physical activity (a walk or jog).

2. *Current Response:* Smoke tobacco, overeat, and drink an excessive amount of coffee.
   Alternative Response: Take a bath or shower, then practice deep breathing or meditation.
3. *Current Response:* Become irritable and use abusive language.
   Alternative Response: Take a time-out to consider options, then redirect activities to improve mood.

This process of redefining responses continues until the leader feels confident that group members have mastered this skill. Once clients spontaneously identify alternative responses without leader intervention, the focus shifts to additional strategies for managing stress.

The next strategy challenges clients to reactivate their inner child. We are indoctrinated from an early age to accept responsibility and "strive to do good." This philosophy, although highly conducive to upward mobility, robs us of our child's view of the world. In our struggle to become, we forget to be! Locked in a pattern of seeing only the "next task on the list," we forget how to play. When life loses its ability to excite and stimulate us, and becomes an unending series of events to endure, stress overload, the inappropriate expression of anger, and relapse are guaranteed results. Reactivating our inner child allows us to reverse this process, inoculating us against stress.

A playful attitude and sense of humor go far in helping to combat irrational thoughts. Ellis (1977, 1987b) recommends the application of rational, humorous songs to attack self-defeating attitudes. Miller, Gorski, and Miller (1982) also promote the use of laughter, play, music, and humor as effective stress management tools. Indeed, every alcohol and drug abuse conference I have attended includes at least one or two sessions addressing this important topic. Ellis et al. (1988) also identify the value of humor to help us recognize the absurdity of our irrational thoughts. If disturbed thinking stems from taking certain ideas too seriously, it stands to reason that humor might help melt away a grim outlook on life.

I rely primarily on two exercises to help clients reactivate their inner child: the telephone game and singing "Old McDonald Had a Farm." To play the telephone game, clients sit in a circle. The leader whispers in one client's ear a message that is passed from person to person until it travels full circle. The leader plays a critical part in modeling play behavior. When leading this game, I become mischievous and playful, encouraging clients to suspend their concerns about looking ridiculous—after all, being silly is part of the fun! My favorite message, since it provides many opportunities for confusion, is "The fireman called his black-and-white spotted dog, climbed into his red fire truck, and raced to put out the raging fire." The message is deliberately long so clients cannot possibly end with up with the "correct answer." Common final responses include: "The dog peed on a fire hydrant." "A red dog put out the fire." "A man had a spotted dog." "A man ran a race with a dog." This game accomplishes several goals:

1. Generates spontaneous laughter among group members
2. Encourages cooperative play
3. Challenges the myth that "it has to be right to be good"
4. Allows clients to examine self-talk messages that limit playful behavior

Once the message comes full circle, clients share their experiences. Most admit enjoyment, but also report feeling embarrassed about what others might think. This leads into the second exercise, singing "Old McDonald Had a Farm." The leader selects someone to start the song (Nobody ever volunteers!). Each member adds a new animal or object to the farm, and the group sings the choruses together. The most creative group I facilitated had 15 clients, making it difficult to remember all the animals and objects named. Clients kept the song moving by making funny faces and mimicking sounds produced by animals and objects mentioned in each chorus. Their response was so enthusiastic, we disrupted other groups concurrently meeting in the clinic! The group ended with laughter and a feeling of uniqueness, since other groups had not experienced this activity. Members of my group later reported that clients from other groups were envious because it sounded like we were having so much fun!

These play activities (and countless others too numerous to mention) help clients reexamine their beliefs about appropriate versus inappropriate adult behavior. The pleasure clients express regarding their ability to play and enjoy childhood games encourages them to experiment beyond group boundaries. They learn that play temporarily suspends responsibilities, replenishing energy reserves. Humor, a component of play, serves a similar purpose. By interrupting the flow of negative energy, at least temporarily, humor allows us to release ourselves from the directive "be right and do good." Leader modeling is critical when teaching this intervention; therefore, a story from my personal life demonstrates humor in action.

LEADER EXAMPLE: THE MUDDY DOG BLUES

We all have pet peeves, and mine is having a muddy dog charge across a freshly mopped floor. My children, like most children, are oblivious to the consequences of mixing a muddy dog with a clean floor. I generally respond with lectures and ominous looks, hoping to ward off repeat performances. One night, as our dog charged through, my oldest son intervened, saying, "Wait Mom! Before you say anything I want to do my impression of you when the dog tracks in mud." He put on a performance worthy of Caesar's Palace! His rendition left me laughing so hard tears streamed down my face. The tension dissolved as I recalled my own guidelines: "Will anyone die from this experience? Will the world end?" Since the answer to both questions was no, I redirected my anger and moved on to the next adventure.

Following this example, clients participate in role plays, applying humor to stressful situations identified by group members. Although humor successfully defuses anger in many situations, it does not work in every circumstance. In situations where others fail to respond favorably, humor can be used to redirect our own response choices and prevent power struggles. The session concludes with a review of directives essential for effective stress management:

1. Heed your parents' advice: A healthy diet, adequate rest, exercise, and a support network do wonders to help minimize the disabling impact of stress. It also reduces the temptation to take it out on others or use stress as a "convenient excuse to relapse."
2. Maintain a positive attitude and remain open to new ideas and experiences. Stress can mean crisis *or* opportunity. Make stress work for rather than against you.

3. Avoid becoming too serious. Make funny faces, skip down the street, play a childhood game. Take breaks from responsibility. This replenishes reserves, and prepares us to cope with stressful situations.
4. Resist the temptation to compare yourself with others. There is no right or wrong way to approach adversity, only differences in how we view and resolve it.
5. Monitor your self-talk. When negative messages creep in, make conscious efforts to rechannel your thoughts in a positive direction. Our thoughts are a powerful resource for managing stress once we learn to harness and direct them.
6. Remember you have the right to set your own pace. Asking for what you want or need and learning to say no are formidable allies in the war against stress.
7. Sidestep the urge to reject help during times of extreme stress. Pride becomes an excuse to play Atlas. Since no person can stand alone in all situations, this attitude wields a deadly blow to sobriety.
8. Finally, and most important, be your own best friend. Selfishly guard your peace of mind and take active steps to create an environment that promotes happiness. Until you accomplish this objective, quality sobriety is an unattainable dream.

13

Managing Resentments

Chapter 13 concludes Part 2 of the anger management-relapse prevention training program. This final module of action strategies for change concentrates on chronic anger, more commonly known as resentment. The theoretical constructs defining rational-emotive and cognitive-behavioral therapies, combined with my conviction that self-esteem plays a critical role in both relapse and recovery, provide a framework for Session 12. A primary objective is to reemphasize the combined effect feelings, thoughts, cognitions, and self-esteem play in the anger-relapse cycle, especially for individuals exhibiting symptoms of chronic anger. A working definition of chronic anger provides a starting point for this task.

Wolf (1988) describes chronic anger as a fixation on painful or humiliating memories from the past. These memories are stockpiled, generating hostile reactions when individuals are confronted with situations that remind them of the past. This hostility provokes an automatic, unrelenting compulsion to replay negative memories over and over again. Each negative remembrance strengthens the individual's conviction that life has cheated him or her out of his or her dreams and aspirations. This self-destructive thought process erodes self-esteem and is often used to justify relapse.

Daley (1988) identifies chronic anger as a condition stemming from inadequate coping skills. When individuals lack skills necessary to express and resolve anger emanating from emotional pain, loss, and divergent points of view, they resort to self-defeating patterns of behavior. Daley contends that increased awareness of unresolved anger, recognition that anger is a problem from within, and acquisition of cognitive and behavioral strategies to appropriately redirect it are critical to interrupting the anger-relapse cycle.

Potter-Efron and Potter-Efron (Potter-Efron, 1990; Potter-Efron, P., & Potter-Efron, 1991; Potter-Efron & Potter-Efron, 1989, 1991a, 1991b) define chronic anger as a symptom of ineffective communication skills. Chronic anger becomes a mechanism for controlling others, maintaining the status quo, creating emotional distance, and defending against shame and other negative feelings. Although it has deleterious effects on relationships, it becomes the emotional glue that holds them together. This clinical team recommends a number of intervention strategies for working with chronically angry clients. First, the clinician must respect the client's right to be angry. This validates anger as a normal, healthy reaction to life's disappointments. An exploration of the etiology of particular anger responses and an emphasis on productive redirection of anger are also critical elements of successful intervention. Finally, when therapists model appropriate responses to anger, clients are more willing to attempt behavior change. If the therapist acknowledges his or her own anger, and works to productively resolve it, these actions will promote a higher degree of credibility, thereby enhancing the therapist's ability to elicit behavior change from others.

Potter-Efron and Potter-Efron (1991a) further describe chronic anger as a mood-altering experience that fosters physical and psychological addiction to anger. The individual develops an automatic pattern of response that begins with negative thoughts (habitually seeing life from a cynical perspective), escalates to emotional extremism, and culminates in impulsive, exaggerated behaviors. The secondary gains gleaned from this experience (a naturally occurring, chemically induced high, a feeling of righteous superiority, the ability to influence others' mood and behavior, and avoidance of personal responsibility for actions and consequences) reinforce the use of anger to justify destructive response choices, including relapse.

Finally, Gorski and Miller (1986) identify chronic anger as a byproduct of the sensitivity to stress characteristic during post-acute withdrawal. Because individuals in early recovery frequently have difficulty distinguishing low- and high-stress situations, a seemingly insignificant event may elicit a disproportionate response. The cumulative effect of repeated misperceptions and overreactions is chronic anger, which may indeed engender "stuck points" as clients make transitions from one developmental stage to the next during the recovery process. Unless identified and successfully redirected, chronic anger fosters a cycle of denial, avoidance, overreaction, confusion, depression, loss of control, and, finally, active relapse.

Once chronic anger is defined, Session 12 turns to a review of factors contributing to resentments. Figure 7 is drawn on the board to graphically depict resentment as a dynamic process, not an independently occurring phenomenon. Clients are informed that the first ingredient of resentment is an action or remark generated by self or others. Once a remark or action is initiated, it is subjected to an evaluation process. This complex process, which occurs in a matter of seconds, is influenced by several factors. First, past experiences shape our interpretations of the action's or remark's intent. If the current situation triggers memories of a past event that was painful or distasteful, the individual's response is likely to be hostile or avoidant. Conversely, if memories of a past event similar to the current situation are positive, the individual's response is likely to be nondefensive and cooperative.

Second, the current state of an individual's self-esteem plays a role in the evaluation process. If I ascribe to an internal frame of reference when determining my value and credibility, the remarks and actions of others can be construed as "their stuff," and my own negative cognitions viewed as a self-defeating response choice that can be interrupted and modified. If, however, my frame of reference stems from external sources, I am likely to personalize these same actions or remarks and develop a sense of hopelessness or persecution that assumes the form of chronic anger.

Third, the nature and quality of the relationship has a significant impact on the interpretive process. When the relationship involves other people, variables such as the length of the relationship, the intensity of attachment, and the congruence or incongruence in beliefs, values, and goals influence our thoughts and response choices. When the relationship only involves interactions with oneself, variables such as perception of personal value and purpose, beliefs regarding one's ability to affect outcomes, and the congruence or incongruence of current

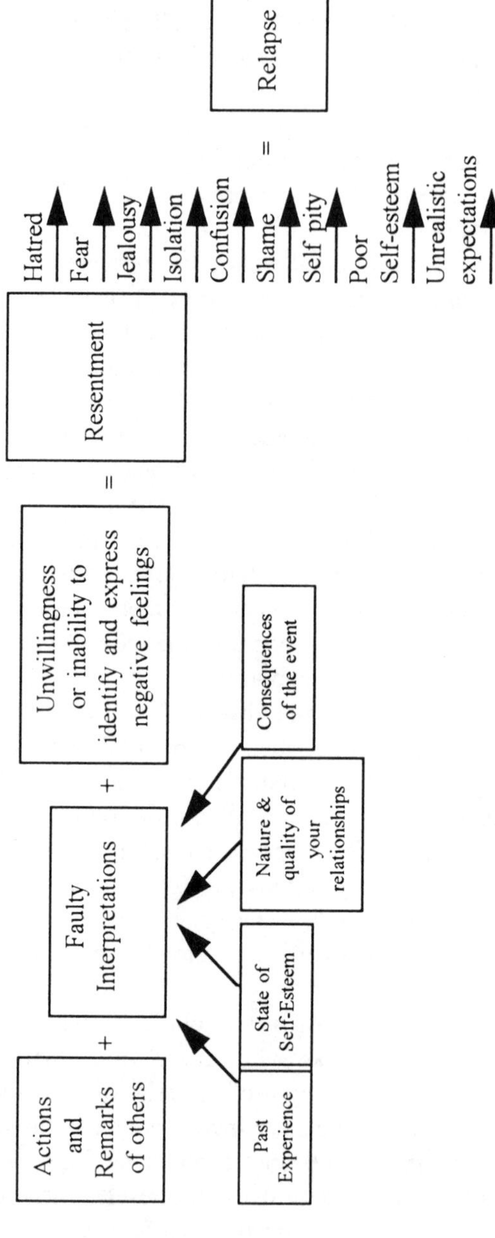

Figure 7. Understanding Resentments

behavior when compared with long-standing values and beliefs become important predictors in the outcome of interpretations.

An additional variable complicating this process is the individual's willingness/unwillingness and ability/inability to openly identify and address negative feelings and cognitions emerging from interpretations of actions and remarks of self or others. If an individual is unable or unwilling to acknowledge his or her distress, interpretations remain subjective, because the individual does not solicit feedback from others regarding the accuracy or inaccuracy of specific interpretations. The vacuum created by this process fosters additional negative feelings and cognitions, resulting in chronic anger. Since the individual either cannot or will not release this anger, he or she misses opportunities to reframe experiences, correct misperceptions, and modify response choices. The outcome is the activation of a myriad of self-defeating feelings, thoughts, and response choices, which, for individuals in recovery, ultimately lead to relapse.

Finally, the consequences that actions or remarks generate in individuals' lives play a role in the evolutionary process of resentment. If an individual experiences painful, embarrassing, or costly consequences related to a specific action or remark, he or she is more likely to succumb to resentment. An example illustrates this point. If an employee makes an error and is flagrantly corrected in front of peers, the potential for resentment is much higher than if the mistake is addressed in private. Receiving a reprimand in the presence of others creates embarrassment and draws negative attention to the individual being admonished. Far-reaching consequences might include peer harassment and hostile exchanges, especially if the nature of peer relationships is competitive or conflicted. This greatly increases the potential for resentments directed both toward one's boss and peers involved in hostile exchanges. An extreme reaction might even involve the chastised individual's premature termination of employment ("To hell with all of you, I quit!"). Receiving a reprimand in private, although uncomfortable, rarely results in embarrassment and does not generate the peer-driven dynamics present in the open exchange. Resentment is unnecessary, since no far-reaching negative consequences arise. The individual simply corrects the mistake and moves on to the next activity.

During this review of factors contributing to resentments, clients can readily identify sources of their resentments, but frequently lack insight regarding the dynamics perpetuating their continuance. A discussion of five factors that transform anger into resentments helps clarify this issue: fear of abandonment, feeling threatened, learned helplessness, secondary gains, and the dilemma, "we don't know how to let go."

1. *Fear of abandonment.* We believe the open and honest expression of feelings and needs will lead to rejection. Ellis (1987a) identifies shame and self-blame as primary sources of emotional disturbance. This is especially true for individuals struggling to overcome chemical dependence. Years of negative feelings, self-defeating thoughts, poor self-esteem, and unproductive response choices have damaged relationships both with oneself and others. Layers of emotional pain arising from multiple losses along the way create a sense that one's debts are so high that no amount of penance can wipe the slate clean. This destructive cognitive process, coupled with inadequate communication skills, leads to faulty interpretations, emotional overreaction, and resentment. The individual may have legitimate reasons to feel angry; however, fear of abandonment and lack of communication skills prevent its productive expression.

A dangerous side-effect of this process is relapse. When chronic anger remains unresolved it intensifies, much like steam in a pressure cooker. A pressure cooker, when properly operated, facilitates fast, efficient meal preparation. If, however, the operator fails to heed safety instructions, serious injuries result. Anger creates similar reactions. When openly identified and addressed, anger is defused, preventing the unhealthy buildup of negative emotions. If suppressed, it severely limits our ability to accurately assess others' behavior. The consequence, in many instances, is an escalation of abandonment fears. In an attempt to preempt abandonment, the individual terminates interaction or severs relationship ties before the other party gets a chance to respond. Unfortunately, this emotional overreaction almost always produces negative results and, thus, a reason to relapse.

2. *Feeling threatened.* We fear the vulnerability that self-disclosures create. Because substance abusers' frame of reference for defining communication are the unwritten rules "Don't talk, don't trust, don't feel" (Black & Bucky, 1986; Wegscheider, 1981; Wegscheider-Cruse, 1976; Woititz, 1983), the suggestion that feelings and needs should be openly identified and addressed is both foreign and terrifying. The uncomfortably familiar pattern of negative feelings, self-defeating cognitions, self-flagellation, resentment, and relapse is a known entity. Despite the pain it creates, familiarity with this repertoire of responses makes it difficult to relinquish them. The possibility of openly expressing one's innermost feelings and thoughts creates an acute sense of vulnerability. This action prompts the realization that in order for change to occur, both strengths and weaknesses must be identified and specific behaviors targeted for modification. Fear of losing the only identity they have ever known is often so great that many individuals refuse to initiate the steps necessary to facilitate recovery.

An analogy is used to help combat the all-or-none thinking that typically arises at this point during the session. I ask clients to envision an artichoke. The tastiest part of this vegetable is its heart. In order to enjoy this part of the artichoke, one must painstakingly work through many layers of leaves. Learning to show vulnerability is much the same. Most people would not even consider approaching a total stranger and revealing their most intimate secrets (unless, of course, that stranger is a therapist!). The revelation of self is a process of unveiling various layers of ourselves, bit by bit, as trust and familiarity grow. Emphasis is placed on the fact that each of us has control over how much and how fast we self-disclose. This built-in safety feature guarantees that we alone choose whether we jump in the pool naked, or with all our clothes on, or something in between.

3. *Learned helplessness.* We come to believe we are powerless over the direction of our lives and see no hope for change. Studies conducted with laboratory animals (Maier, Seligman, & Solomon, 1969; Seligman, 1975) support the hypothesis that if an organism perceives itself incapable of eliciting change, it will cease to initiate attempts and passively submit to aversive stimuli even in the presence of opportunities for escape. These early studies demonstrated that after repeated exposure to inescapable aversive stimuli, when these same animals were exposed to escapable aversive stimuli they either did not initiate escape responses or were slow and inept at escaping. In essence, they learned that termination of an aversive stimulus was independent of their behavior. This lesson was so powerful, they continued to function as if helpless even when presented with opportunities to interrupt an aversive stimulus.

A later study (Abramson, Seligman, & Teasdale, 1978) demonstrated similar responses in humans. The belief that one lacks control over reinforcing variables was sufficient to create learned helplessness in animals. When applied to humans, a second variable plays a critical role in the acquisition of learned helplessness: the explanation identified to explain their loss of control. Individuals in situations perceived as uncontrollable who also believe this loss of control is permanent, not temporary, are more at risk for learned helplessness. Likewise, individuals who believe their loss of control is due to internal factors (self-esteem, character flaws, personality style) carry a higher risk than do those who perceive their loss of control as stemming from environmental factors. Finally, if individuals identify this loss of control as a global experience that affects many aspects of their lives, as opposed to one or two specific areas of functioning, they are more likely to manifest symptoms of learned helplessness.

To help clients gain a better grasp of this concept, they are referred back to Session 5 (see Chapter 6), which introduced the role of self-talk, both in relapse and recovery. They are reminded that restructuring longstanding patterns of thought, although difficult, is attainable. The key to preventing learned helplessness and the activation of the anger-relapse cycle is early identification and interruption of destructive cognitive processes and replacement with more productive response choices.

4. *Secondary gains.* Resentments provide payoffs: Individuals frequently use chronic anger as an excuse for certain behavior and its consequences (Bootzin, 1980). "I am angry, therefore out of control, so I should not be held accountable for my actions." A second payoff is that both covert and overt expressions of resentment attract attention (Bootzin, 1980). Whether I withdraw, creating a "walking on eggshells" atmosphere, or become loud and obnoxious, the result is the same: Attention is focused on me! The uneasiness created by active resentment heightens others' anxiety to the point that they will do anything to break the tension. This transference of power (my behavior affects your mood and response choices) reinforces the use of resentment to achieve desired goals without having to negotiate or compromise.

A good example is a chemically dependent family in which one member is diagnosed as alcohol dependent. This individual is irritable and edgy, always threatening to drink "if you guys don't stop bugging me." The family, unless participating in treatment, frequently assumes the victim role, allowing this person to hold them hostage. The alcoholic has the best of both worlds: If he or she drinks, blame is projected onto family members. If he or she maintains sobriety, the threat of relapse continues to control other family members. This process reinforces chronic anger, creating high denial and resistance when the individual is challenged to change. A favorite rationale of the addict/alcoholic is "Why should I change? Things are fine just like they are." Other family members rarely paint such a rosy picture.

5. *"We don't know how to let go."* We never learned to explore, process, and let go of resentments. Again, chemically dependent individuals, functioning under the unwritten rules "Don't talk, don't trust, don't feel" (Black & Bucky, 1986; Wegscheider, 1981; Wegscheider-Crus, 1976; Woititz, 1983), experience a poverty of communication skills. Distortions in reality and the concepts of normal versus abnormal and healthy versus unhealthy make it virtually impossible for them to reach accurate interpretations of the actions and remarks around them. The confusion experienced when attempts are initiated to resolve chronic anger frequently activate a fear-avoidance response, verbalized as "It doesn't really matter anyway." Two analogies are used to help clients understand how destructive unresolved anger can be.

The first example involves a discussion about volcanoes. Inactive volcanoes often present a serene, innocuous appearance. Mount Saint Helens was indeed a beautiful mountain, providing a breathtaking backdrop for a nearby lake. Looking at this mountain, one would never guess that a gradual buildup of heat and molten rock was steadily increasing its internal pressure. Because the mountain had not yet erupted, no crevasses were available to vent off steam and maintain a reasonable internal pressure. As time passed, the mountain's internal pressure continued to increase, until one day it dramatically exploded, creating devastating consequences for the surrounding communities. This process also occurs in the presence of chronic anger and relapse. Unless opportunities are identified *and* activated to interrupt the buildup of negative feelings and thoughts, the consequence will ultimately be destructive displays of anger (both implosions and explosions) and relapse.

The second example involves icebergs. An iceberg is an enormous mass of compressed ice, typically found in the colder oceans of the world. Although the visible portion of an iceberg may appear quite large, in reality the bulk of this massive structure is hidden beneath the sea. The depth of an iceberg is of no consequence to the captain of a ship. Since it can be seen from a distance, the defensive action is simply to steer around it. The circumstance is quite different if the vessel in question is a submarine. Unlike the ship captain who can see the iceberg and steer around it, a submarine captain must rely on sonar to determine the depth and dimensions of icebergs along the submarine's plotted course. Accurate and timely communications from the submarine's sonar operator are critical to the safety of the vessel. Chronic anger creates a dilemma for significant others that is similar to the challenge faced by the submarine captain. Individuals rarely display the bulk of their anger. Much like an iceberg, the bulk of it is stored deep within an individual's psyche. This presents no problem for strangers and casual acquaintances, who can simply steer around the individual when visible signs of anger are detected. Unfortunately, significant others are confronted with the same dilemma the submarine captain faces: They depend on accurate and timely information from their loved one to determine appropriate courses of action. When this information is withheld or distorted, individuals involved in these relationships experience negative consequences (e.g., estranged, conflicted, or fragmented relationships, somatic or emotional symptoms of distress, relapse). These analogies heighten awareness of the powerful and destructive influence unresolved anger can have on recovery.

After reviewing these factors, clients learn to discriminate between three types of resentment: self-directed, outward-directed (projected), and other-generated. The first type of resentment is self-directed, involving hostility directed toward oneself. Factors generating this response include, but are not limited to, consequences of addictive behavior: lost relationships, declining health, legal entanglements, unemployment, financial distress, loss of self-esteem, and losing the respect of others.

Self-directed resentments focus on past mistakes. Individuals caught in this destructive cycle expend huge amounts of energy on self-recrimination. The reality that past events cannot be undone is ignored as they obsess over failures to "be right" or "do good." This type of resentment is poison to recovery! It reinforces self-defeating behavior and provides a convenient excuse for relapse. Examples of negative self-talk perpetuating this behavior include the following:

- "I am a failure; things will never change."
- "I've burned all my bridges; nobody will ever trust me again."

- "I'll never live down the past; my whole life has been wasted."
- "If only I had stopped using/drinking sooner."
- "It's too late; I can never undo all the damage I created."

These inflammatory self-statements set the process of relapse in motion. Since there is no hope of influencing the past, individuals replay past mistakes over and over, attempting to find some previously overlooked item to magically open the door to forgiveness. What individuals afflicted with self-directed resentments fail to realize is that the magic switch needed to stop this process is inside their heads! A case example will help illustrate this point.

CASE STUDY: MR. Y.

Mr. Y. is a middle-aged man with a 25-year history of alcohol dependence. He has been married and divorced five times, has children by several wives that he neither supports nor maintains contact with, and has so enraged extended family members that they refuse to talk to him or allow him to visit. Mr. Y. also has a long history of employment failures. He identified 25 jobs in the past 15 years; most were lost due to absenteeism, anger dyscontrol (yelling at bosses, walking off jobs), and failure to meet deadlines on projects. He has also had his fair share of legal difficulties. Mr. Y. has three driving while intoxicated charges and in excess of 20 public intoxication charges. As Mr. Y.'s addiction has progressed, he has witnessed the deaths of multiple "associates" from alcohol-related causes. When this client entered treatment, he expressed a sense of hopelessness and defeat. He verbalized that treatment was his last hope to get control of his life.

Intervention

Since Mr. Y. has been sober for 3 months, medical detoxification was deemed unnecessary. He was enrolled in an outpatient clinic and scheduled to attend a variety of groups three nights a week. This client was initially very pessimistic, and the underlying theme of his interactions with others was a sense of resignation. In process group he repeatedly reviewed stories from his past but made no attempt to modify behaviors that prevented him from moving forward. This client was placed in the anger management-relapse prevention training program in hopes of redirecting his self-defeating feelings, thoughts, and response choices.

Mr. Y. was assisted in identifying the specific messages that repeatedly triggered negative self-talk. He was asked to keep a daily journal so the dynamics driving this pattern could be recognized and interrupted. His journal revealed that fear of abandonment and learned helplessness were predominant forces in his self-directed resentment. He had developed unrealistic expectations of himself and others, thereby inevitably setting himself up for failure by withdrawing from supports, then chastising himself for being unable to establish and maintain meaningful relationships. Heavy emphasis was placed on recognizing self-defeating cognitions and replacing them with more productive alternatives. He was instructed in the combined application of time-out, detouring self-talk, and problem solving to generate alternative response choices. He was also encouraged to review his current patterns of communication and to work toward a more assertive presentation of feelings and needs. Finally, he was asked to maintain a here-and-now focus. When he felt himself dwelling on past or future events, he was instructed to make a journal entry to identify the circumstances that triggered this shift in orientation.

Outcome

Mr. Y.'s progress was tedious and slow. He made many false starts and initially stormed out of sessions, expressing defeat. He was encouraged to tackle small issues first and work toward resolving more complex cognitive patterns once he experienced enough successes to foster a sense of hopefulness. The group was critical to his recovery, since peers provided both confrontation when he attempted to avoid responsibility for modifying his response choices and support when he made progress toward redirecting negative thoughts and response choices. When he terminated treatment, he displayed moderate improvement in interrupting self-defeating cognitions. He was cautioned that continued application and refinement of skills, both in the anger process group (discussed in Chapter 14) and in daily life situations, would be critical in establishing long-term behavior change.

The second type of resentment is outward-directed. This reaction is based on negative perceptions of others' intentions. Energies are channeled into blaming others for our problems.

- "If only you would/would not have . . ."
- "If you really loved me you would/wouldn't . . ."
- "Since you really don't care about me anyway . . ."
- "The world is a setup for failure; everywhere I go I run into people who use and abuse me."

Emotional reactions generated by this type of resentment mask genuine issues, leading to the depletion of energy reserves before the "real problem" is even addressed. Secondary gains and enabling behaviors of significant others further complicate this destructive process.

Individuals employing outward-directed resentments steadfastly resist attempts to confront the illogical nature of their behavior. Because they successfully manipulate their environment with few negative consequences, it is difficult to identify valid reasons for behavior change. Since significant others play a critical role in perpetuating this cycle, multifamily group therapy is highly recommended. Teaching family members and friends to avoid accepting responsibility for the addict or alcoholic's behavior forces the client to assess and own his or her behavior and allows family members to escape from their roles as emotional hostages. The K. family is a classic example of this dynamic in action.

CASE STUDY: THE K. FAMILY

Mr. and Mrs. K. are both in their mid-80s. Their 45-year-old son has been living with them for the past 3 years. The presenting problem was the parents' distress regarding their son's abuse of alcohol. When treatment began, he had been unemployed for 11 months and drank on a daily basis, despite his parents' discomfort with this behavior. This adult son had multiple failed treatment attempts, and during the initial interview identified little interest in changing his current circumstances. His parents, in great contrast, experienced significant distress as they observed a gradual but steady decline in his physical condition and mental health.

This family came into treatment requesting assistance in resolving this dilemma. The parents both professed great love for this son; however, they indicated that no matter what they did he became hostile or defensive, blaming them for his inability to achieve happiness. They repeatedly loaned him money that was never repaid, allowed him to drink at home for fear he would kill himself or others if he drank elsewhere, and refrained from asking him to contribute either energy or funds toward the maintenance of their home. The younger Mr. K. indicated that he only lived at home because he was unable to hold a job and that his parents should stop bugging him and be grateful that he even agreed to come in for treatment. His hostility toward his parents increased after they chastised him for throwing a party in their absence and paying for it with their credit cards. When they attempted to justify their displeasure, he stated, "Isn't that what parents are for? If you don't love me anymore I'll just leave!" They reported past attempts to set limits but always relented when he became defensive or accused them of not loving him.

Intervention

Since this enmeshed pattern of behavior between parents and child was deeply entrenched, the family was enrolled in a multifamily group. The younger Mr. K. was concurrently enrolled in the anger management-relapse prevention training program. The first step in treatment involved education regarding addiction and addictive behaviors. Information about the impact on family members and about typical response styles was also presented. The K.'s had great resistance to "abandoning" their son, and therefore were assisted with reality testing. A pertinent question that raised considerable anxiety was "I know you love him very much and want to take care of him; however, you are both in your mid-80s and won't live forever. If he does not learn to take responsibility for himself now, what will happen to him after you're gone?" The K.'s had considered this reality previously, but always managed to avoid dealing with it directly. They were also aided in identifying the negative self-talk that fueled their overextensions of support. Common themes included the following: "It must be our fault that he turned out this way, so we have to help him." "He is our son; blood is thicker than water, no matter what." The group was very supportive in helping the K.'s develop a plan so they could be supportive without continuing to contribute to their son's addiction.

The younger Mr. K. identified his self-defeating patterns of thinking and behavior in the anger management-relapse prevention training program. He acknowledged great fear that his parents would abandon him; however, he felt unable to express this fear, and so reacted with hostility and resistance. He was aided in developing more assertive communication skills that he then applied during multifamily group. Peer support was also vital to this client's treatment. His low self-esteem, fear of abandonment, and impoverished communication style had created a pattern of reaction-withdrawal-relapse that heightened his anger toward his parents, whom he felt did not understand.

Outcome

During the course of multifamily group, the K. family developed a set of ground rules that all members found acceptable. The younger Mr. K. agreed to stay in treatment and to refrain from drinking alcohol. He also agreed to pursue either retraining or employment so he could begin establishing skills necessary for independent living. The parents set firm limits regarding their son's need to contribute both financially and physically to the upkeep of their home. They expressed genuine surprise when their son agreed to these terms.

The members of this family developed more effective communication skills and were all surprised to learn that they shared common fears and goals. This open expression of feelings (which occurred over a period of 6 months) gradually eroded the younger Mr. K.'s resentment toward his parents, as he identified his role in his current unhappiness. When the family left treatment, they had developed a healthier pattern of communication, and the conflict that precipitated treatment had dissipated to a more manageable level.

The third type of resentment involves hostility others direct toward you. This encompasses anger harbored by individuals adversely affected by behaviors occurring during active phases of the addictive process. Their goal is to punish you for wrongdoing. This type of resentment is especially difficult to withstand because situations cannot be recalled and corrected. Making amends is frequently impossible, even when individuals are willing, due to a lack of available opportunities.

Client responses to this type of resentment include threatening relapse or actual relapse episodes, abusive behavior, and withdrawal. The resulting power struggles intensify hostility, diminishing opportunities for successful problem resolution. At the other end of the continuum, clients overcompensate, desperately attempting to please the offended party. This sets the stage for double-bind dynamics: Significant others demand corrective action and the client eagerly complies. Instead of generating the anticipated response, this ingratiating behavior elicits further attacks. Unless arrested, this cycle places the recovering addict or alcoholic at serious risk for relapse and leaves significant others feeling angry and abused. The experiences of Ms. N. provide a clear example of this type of resentment.

CASE STUDY: MS. N.

Ms. N. is a 38-year-old addict with a 20-year history of polydrug abuse. Her addiction has resulted in the failure of three marriages, the loss of custody of her four children, the inability to secure stable employment, and animosity from her extended family members and friends. She has one lifelong friend who has expressed such anger over Ms. N.'s drug-seeking escapades that she has terminated the relationship. Ms. N., with 6 months of sobriety under her belt, is determined to "win back" the love of this friend, no matter what the cost. She continues to call this friend and to drop by the friend's house for visits. This individual consistently spurns her and has given no indication that she is interested in repairing the relationship. Ms. N.'s deep distress over the probable loss of this relationship has brought her perilously close to relapse on several occasions. Her identified goal is to develop a strategy to win back her friend once and for all.

Intervention

Ms. N.'s deep distress over losing this significant relationship obviously hooks into an iceberg of other experiences. While enrolled in the anger management-relapse prevention training program, she discovered a theme of abandonment that stemmed from childhood. She had been raised in an alcoholic home and was frequently shuffled from relative to relative, since her parents felt unable to care for her. She escaped into marriage at a young age and continued to select unsuitable partners, leading to three additional episodes of "abandonment." The loss of her children, due to her active substance abuse and inability to maintain stable employment, was the ultimate blow. The only long-term relationship she had left was this now-estranged friend. Thus, a tremendous amount of energy was invested in salvaging what she perceived as her last link to her past.

During the course of her therapy, Ms. N. explored these dynamics, and the group helped her identify factors that kept her stuck in this no-win situation. Ms. N. not only experienced tremendous abandonment fears, but also received secondary gains from pursuing her cause. It allowed her to gain sympathy from others and to avoid addressing her own issues and the need for change, and it saved her from having to invest time and energy developing a new support network. The group provided opportunities for her to grieve the multiple losses attached to her addiction, to identify strengths she could use to develop new patterns of communication, and to obtain support and friendship as she struggled to learn and apply productive response choices. One of her most significant experiences was writing a farewell letter to this friend and reading it in group. She discovered that although her friend had not forgiven her, she could be a catalyst in forgiving herself.

Outcome

Initially, Ms. N. refused to let go of this friendship. The more group members prodded her to relinquish this impossible goal, the more tightly she clung to her conviction that she had to regain this friend's trust at all costs. As time passed and she developed a clearer understanding of the dynamics generating her intense reactions, she was able to acknowledge that although tragic, this friendship had ended. She gradually began to venture out to Narcotics Anonymous meetings with her fellow group members and developed tentative attachments to several of the female group members.

GROUP EXERCISE

Following this discussion of the three primary manifestations of resentment, clients complete a worksheet to explore their own resentments (see Worksheet 9, pp. 186–187). This worksheet helps clients identify and examine personal patterns of expressing and coping with chronic anger. The purpose of this exercise is for clients to challenge existing feelings, thoughts, and response choices. The desired result of this activity is to activate a level of dissonance great enough to initiate behavior change.

The personal resentments worksheet uncovers several recurring themes. The two most frequently identified involve self-directed resentments and resentments that others, angered by the consequences of addiction, direct toward the recovering addict/alcoholic. Clients concede they lack skills to manage the negative feelings and thoughts arising from these sources of hostility. Since the road to relapse is paved with resentments, clients must learn to create a "last free exit" off this toll road. To prepare clients for this challenge, step-by-step strategies for managing each type of resentment are outlined below.

Steps to Overcome Self-Directed Resentments

1. *Identify triggers.* Evaluate factors that occur each time you experience negative self-talk. Where are you? Who are you with? Do negative thoughts arise at particular times of the day or on certain days of the week? Is there a pattern you can identify and modify?
2. *Explore your feelings.* What emotions do self-directed resentments activate? Do sadness, fear, or confusion influence your response choices? Do you feel defeated or out of control? Learning to recognize negative emotions is the first step in letting them go.
3. *Develop strategies to combat self-directed assaults.* Realize that past behaviors cannot be altered. Focus on what can be accomplished, rather than agonizing over what cannot be. Shame-attacking exercises (Ellis & Becker, 1982; Ellis & Harper, 1975) can be learned and practiced in group to reduce deep-seated humiliation and embarrassment generated by behaviors initiated during active addiction.
4. *Strive to forgive yourself.* Separate *you* from *your behavior*. Every individual is intrinsically good, but we all at times make poor choices. Do your best to focus on what is right with you rather than on what is not. Remember that forgiveness is an option, not an expectation, and must be accomplished gradually, and with patience (Smedes, 1984).

Steps in Overcoming Resentments You Hold toward Others

1. *Identify specific issues.* Be precise in defining the "real" issue. Address one issue at a time to prevent derailment from your stated objective(s). By focusing on the problem, rather than the person, opportunities to create mutually satisfying results increase.
2. *Apply detouring self-talk.* Modify your thinking so you can approach issues from a nonjudgmental point of view. Remember that others may not respond in the manner we anticipate. The goal is *not* to convince others to ascribe to our philosophy. Rather, it involves developing the skills necessary to redirect our own behavior when faced with disappointment or regret.
3. *Use "I" statements.* Own your feelings and express them in a manner that reduces defensiveness in others. Remember that personalizing feelings and needs helps others develop a clearer picture of your current situation and reduces resistance, since there is no need to deflect hostile or critical accusations (e.g., instead of saying, "You're a real jerk! If you had any brains you'd know I need some extra attention," try saying, "I'm feeling kind of left out today; can I please have a hug?").
4. *Reframe the resentment.* Shift your thinking. Consider the other person's experience. You may have inadvertently stumbled into a situation where anger is directed toward you but is not about you. Remember that a fearful or confused individual often strikes out when attempting to regain control. Avoid the temptation to take it personally—it may not be personal!
5. *Strive to let go of the past.* Since the past is beyond our control, stop wasting time ruminating about what was and focus on what is. Determine what you need *at this time* to either resolve the resentment or release it and move on.

Steps in Overcoming Resentments Others Hold Against You

1. *Maintain a nondefensive posture.* The temptation to fight hostility with hostility escalates resentments, reducing the possibility of a successful outcome. Remember—you are *only* responsible for your own

behavior. You do not have the power to change the actions or feelings of others.

2. *Make amends when possible.* Accept responsibility for your actions. Apologize and offer to take corrective actions necessary for conflict resolution.
3. *When you are unable to make amends or your efforts are rejected.*
   a. Remember that you cannot alter past behavior.
   b. You cannot change, *nor are you responsible for* changing, the thoughts or behaviors of others.
   c. You *can* modify current and future behaviors in yourself.
4. *Take active steps to move forward in recovery.* Maintain your momentum by encouraging the resentful party to participate in treatment so you can work together to improve interactions. If this individual refuses, continue working on your own issues. The best possible outcome is that your shifts in thinking and behavior will eventually sway others' thinking and behavior. The worst possible outcome is that you may lose relationships; however, treatment will provide the necessary insight and skills to help you avoid relapse during this period of loss and adjustment.

Although intrigued by this review of interventions, clients remain skeptical since change requires considerable investments of time and energy. A reminder that resentments also consume time and energy helps eliminate these doubts. Additional reassurance is gleaned from the following analogy. Clients are instructed to think of the energy contained in a high-voltage power line. When properly harnessed, energy in this line has multiple benefits: It lights our homes, activates our appliances, and allows us to complete daily tasks quickly and efficiently. The same power, if unleashed by virtue of a damaged line, becomes a lethal force.

The energy driving resentments is comparable. Resentments generate intense emotional reactions, sapping strength and distracting us from goal-directed activities. When unresolved, negative energy intensifies, heightening our perception of distress. Calls for energy to combat this distress deplete energy reserves, increasing our susceptibility to stress overload and relapse. The same energy, used to apply constructive interventions, provides avenues for conflict resolution and the maintenance of sobriety.

This comparison provides a fresh perspective on resentments. Clients learn they alone are responsible for directing energy toward a more positive end. Blaming self or others for past behaviors cannot alter this truism, and serves only to entrench denial and elevate relapse potential. By the session's end they understand, and may or may not accept, the reality of this statement. Clients now face a crossroads in recovery: The first road terminates formal treatment, and recovery continues without professional support. The second leads to aftercare, providing opportunities to strengthen and sustain newly acquired skills. Clients are advised to consider these options carefully and select the road that best supports their sobriety. Part 3 will explore aftercare issues and present alternative applications for the anger management-relapse prevention program.

Part 3

Aftercare and Beyond

FOCUS 1: To help clients strengthen and sustain newly acquired coping skills and develop personalized plans for anger management and relapse prevention

FOCUS 2: To present alternative applications for the anger management-relapse prevention training program

14

The Anger Process Group

The anger process group is the brainchild of my clients. Before its inception, clients participated in an 8-week anger management-relapse prevention training program, then continued recovery in traditional treatment groups. Clients completing the program expressed a desire for more extensive training. The addition of four training sessions accommodated this request. Clients reacted favorably; however, they continued to verbalize a need to practice newly acquired skills. In response, I conducted a survey to assess experiences clients perceived necessary to meet this need. The results of this survey gave rise to the anger process group.

A long-term endeavor, the anger process group is open to clients who have completed the 12-week training program. Clients determine the length of time they wish to invest in this group, with a minimum commitment of 4 weeks and a maximum of 36. Voluntary in nature, the group attracts individuals seriously committed to sobriety and anger management. The premise that cognitions and behavior are learned and therefore can be challenged and replaced with alternative responses provides the framework upon which this group is built (Annis, 1986; Annis & Davis, 1987a, 1987b; Bandura, 1969, 1971a, 1971b; Barlow, 1978; Beck, 1976, 1988; Beck et al., 1979; Bellack & Hersen, 1985; Daley, 1988; Ellis, 1973, 1985; Ellis & Becker, 1982; Ellis & Dryden, 1987; Ellis & Greiger, 1977; Ellis & Harper, 1975; Ellis et al., 1988; Ellis & Whiteley,

1979; Mahoney, 1974; Mahoney & Thoresen, 1974; Marlatt & Gordon, 1985; Meichenbaum, 1977; Thoresen & Coates, 1980; Walen et al., 1980; Wessler & Wessler, 1980). Group discussion, role plays, and homework assignments, with subsequent peer review, reinforce this concept.

The primary goal of the aftercare program is to strengthen and sustain clients' newly developed skills. The objectives below facilitate achievement of this goal:

1. Clients will learn to differentiate between self and behavior.
2. Peer support will provide a mechanism for confronting rationalizations and eroding denial.
3. Role plays, group discussion, and homework assignments will reinforce newly acquired skills.
4. The dynamics underlying current responses will be identified so alternative behaviors can be substituted.
5. Positive feedback from peers and group leader(s) will support long-term behavior change.
6. Greater control over personal response choices will promote positive self-regard.
7. Participation in group exercises and homework assignments will instill self-discipline.
8. Clients will develop more realistic expectations regarding relationship issues.

Few clients willingly expose themselves to in-depth explorations of their feelings, thoughts, and response choices, especially when the goal is to initiate change. Therefore, the initial anger process group began with a scant three members. These pioneers faithfully attended weekly sessions for 9 months. They concentrated on learning to anticipate counterproductive responses and implement appropriate alternatives. Group sessions relied heavily on client entries in the anger management-relapse prevention journal. These entries helped clients identify alternative response choices, which were then role-played in vitro to enhance successful application beyond group parameters.

As the anger process group evolved, members described their experiences in it to traditional treatment groups, paving the way for others to join. The treatment team was also instrumental in channeling clients into this group. Team members occasionally identified clients not planning to continue in aftercare and enticed them to join on a quasi-voluntary basis, with the caveat of permission to withdraw after 4 weeks. During the years I led this group, none of my quasi-voluntary clients withdrew prematurely. Even more surprising, they ALL elected to remain enrolled for the 36 week maximum!

Helping clients differentiate between self and behavior is a primary objective of the group. Clients generally intertwine these concepts, creating a self-defeating view of themselves and recovery. Accepting the label "bad person" provides clients with an excuse to continue both inappropriate and addictive patterns of behavior. If a person is inherently bad, they rationalize, change is beyond the realm of possibility. The anger process group challenges clients to reject the label "bad person" and replace it with the concept "unproductive response choices." This change in semantics assigns responsibility to the client. By shifting the focus from other to self-directed responsibility for behavior and its consequences, clients discover countless opportunities to initiate change.

Peer modeling is essential for the group's success. Modeling has the potential to modify attitudes and introduce new skills by providing opportunities to observe and learn alternative response choices (Bandura, 1969, 1971a, 1971b). Since group members share the common bonds of addiction and anger dyscontrol, peer modeling becomes a powerful catalyst for the acquisition and performance of new skills. Although open-ended, the group has a core of long-term members available for guidance and support. These veteran members are experts at identifying and confronting denial, and peer status affords them far greater credibility than that of the leaders. Mr. C. is an excellent example of peer modeling in action.

Mr. C. enrolled in the group as a quasi-voluntary client. Resistance emanated from him as he stated, "I am only capable of three emotions: angry, pissed-off, and like you see me right now." He dared the group to convince him otherwise. As the weeks went by, Mr. C. became more open, participating in group discussions and role plays. Despite this change in behavior, he remained adamant that he was capable of only three emotions. Group members took it upon themselves to confront this client's belief system. Each time he displayed a new emotion, they provided feedback and support. This peer intervention was so successful that Mr. C. identified *and acknowledged* eight new emotions by the end of his enrollment 9 months later!

A strong correlation exists between understanding the dynamics shaping thoughts and behavior and one's ability to establish lasting change. Participation in a life review helps clients capitalize on this connection. During this review, clients often identify painful childhood memories as triggers for current response choices. Stress, they report, creates an overwhelming sensation of being thrust backward in time to the powerless position of a child. Their fear of being forced to submit to and endure additional abuse distorts perceptions, exaggerating defensive reactions. This reactivity promotes conflict, increasing relapse potential. The group provides a medium for clients to work through and neutralize the impact these memories have on current behavior. Peer support, once again, plays a critical role, since group members know from whence their peers come.

Repetition is a powerful tool in the process of change and is an integral part of each session. Each time a concept is repeated, clients glean additional information useful in modifying current response choices. An occasional disgruntled client will complain, "Jo, we're covering the same material over and over again!" An analogy is offered to allay this malcontentment. Most individuals, at some point during their childhood, learn to ride a bicycle. The tricycle is a standard beginner's vehicle. As skills develop, young riders graduate to a bicycle with training wheels. Finally, the long-awaited day arrives—the training wheels are removed! A number of false starts mark this rite of passage. This analogy helps clients realize that learning to apply alternative responses, like learning to ride a bicycle, *only* occurs when practiced on a regular basis. Attending group, without actively applying what is learned, guarantees regression to previous behaviors.

The work of Gorski and Miller (1986) is also identified to support the belief that follow-up reinforcement is essential to long-term maintenance of sobriety. Clients are reminded that awareness of relapse triggers, skills acquisition to modifying existing response choices, and practice on a daily basis are critical factors both for sobriety and effective management of anger. Initially, this requires involvement in formal recovery programs augmented by community-based support groups. As the length of sobriety increases, formal treatment ends and the individual maintains new thoughts and behavior by attending community support groups. The frequency of attendance is variable, contingent upon individual needs and the levels of harmony and distress individuals experience at different points across time. Failure to develop and participate in a maintenance program significantly increases relapse potential.

A final, and crucial, component of the anger process group involves teaching clients to establish realistic expectations for themselves, their relationships, and recovery. The addictive process, by its very nature, distorts perceptions of reality, leaving clients and their significant others frustrated and confused. Expectations are generally based on faulty perceptions rather than fact, intensifying conflict and providing convenient excuses for relapse or withdrawal from treatment. Peer confrontations and role-play exercises provide reality checks and offer realistic alternatives.

Although clients participate in this group for up to 9 months, they experience anxiety as termination approaches. Frequent concerns include the following:

- "Will I remember what I have learned?"
- "Even if I DO remember, will I be able to successfully apply new skills when challenging situations arise?"
- "What will happen if I get stuck and you are not there to troubleshoot for me?"

I remind clients that by the time discharge arrives they possess the skills necessary for continued success. Reassurances of consultation during the postdischarge transition also alleviate fears. My pioneer group members went so far as to suggest weekly meetings, facilitated by me, of course, at a local coffee shop. I assured them my presence was unnecessary. The remainder of the session focused on helping them develop realistic alternatives. These clients decided to alternate weekly meetings in each other's homes for mutual support. During follow-up contacts, they recounted a successful transition from formal treatment to informal peer support.

Termination is an important aspect of therapy. Therefore, the focus for clients approaching discharge is the potential impact of unresolved issues on long-term sobriety. The leader solicits group feedback regarding graduating members' progress and problem areas for further work. This information establishes priorities for concluding sessions. As a final assignment, clients approaching discharge review their experiences and offers suggestions to remaining members. This review serves two purposes: (1) Exiting clients have opportunities to identify and acknowledge progress, reinforcing their commitment to the maintenance of cognitive and behavioral change, and (2) the successful exploits of exiting members provide modeling for group members continuing in treatment.

Participation in the anger process group enhances clients' abilities to maintain sobriety and appropriately resolve conflicts. The group's ongoing nature provides opportunities to test new feelings, thoughts, and response choices, apply them in real-life settings, then return for feedback and support. My strong beliefs that peer support and repetition form the foundation of successful intervention leads me to urge inclusion of an aftercare program, modeled after the anger process group, when applying materials presented in this book. The final chapter, alternative applications, presents factors precluding compliance with this recommendation.

15

Alternative Applications

As a social worker employed by the Houston Veterans Affairs Medical Center, my client population is limited to military veterans and their significant others. Although I occasionally have opportunities to counsel women, most of my work involves interventions with men. When presenting workshops, two questions always arise: "Can your program be applied to client populations other than veterans?" "Can clients benefit from training if my setting requires me to limit the number of sessions offered?" My response to both questions is YES. This chapter, targeting client populations most frequently identified during training workshops, addresses alternative applications for my program.

One word of caution is offered to enhance successful modification of this program. Regardless of how many sessions you provide, inclusion of sessions to identify triggers and cues and the influence of past experiences on current feelings, thoughts, and response choices is essential. Failure to develop this foundation will sabotage clients' best efforts to acquire and implement action strategies for change. If I cannot recognize the process that drives the anger-relapse cycle, it severely limits my ability to strategically place interventions necessary to interrupt this process. Remember the analogy of the Ferrari: we do not go from 0 to 60 mph in 5.2 seconds; however, if we cannot identify the acceleration process, we will repeatedly find ourselves at 60 mph and have no clue how we got there or what steps we might have taken to prevent its occurrence.

Many of my colleagues work in the private sector, and a common concern is whether the program can be applied to nonveterans. There is nothing unique about a veteran population, beyond the fact that clients served in the armed forces at some point during their life. My clients come from all races, ages, income ranges, and geographic locations. A primary issue when applying the program to nonveteran populations involves the parameter of time. Since my clients are outpatients of a federal institution, I function with considerable latitude regarding the type and duration of services provided. Those of you practicing in the private sector have more restrictive guidelines for service provision.

Several strategies facilitate adaptations of the program to compressed time parameters. When training must be accomplished in 28 days, a typical inpatient length of stay, sessions can be conducted three times weekly. Much like attending summer school, clients receive the same amount of training in a significantly shorter period of time. The anger process group, offered as an aftercare program, is attended postdischarge. The *primary disadvantage* of this approach is the rapid disbursement of information. Clients have limited opportunities for review and practice and may fail to acquire essential skills. This is especially significant if your client population includes individuals experiencing various levels of decompensation upon admission. Precious group time is lost waiting for their symptoms to abate. The *primary advantages* of this approach are a closed group format and the continuity of care aspect the aftercare group provides.

A second option for coping with compacted time frames is the careful selection of sessions most appropriate for your population. When the luxury of offering 12 sessions and a follow-up group are not possible, assess your clients' strengths and weaknesses and design a 4-6 session miniseries. If clients are aggressive and verbally abusive, time-out, detouring self-talk, and managing resentments are critical elements of treatment. When clients exhibit passive-aggressive behaviors, interventions include identification of current communication styles, learning to ask for what you need and to say no, and the effective use of feeling-level statements. The *primary disadvantage* is, of course, access to only a portion of the program. The *advantage*, however, is intensive training designed to deal directly with target behaviors.

A second issue raised in my workshops involves application of the training program to nonaddicted client populations. My pilot group, initiated to address this issue, included five clients with diagnoses of depression, posttraumatic stress disorder (PTSD), and bipolar disorder. None of these clients had *identified* diagnoses of addictive disease when admitted to the group. Educational materials, modified to encompass symptoms of my clients' various disorders, promote recognition of warning signs and prompt application of strategies designed to redirect responses, to prevent regressive behavior.

As clients explored dynamics driving current behaviors, an important discovery surfaced: Three of the five clients without diagnoses of addictive disease had family histories of addictive disease, and *all* admitted periodic drug or alcohol abuse to diminish symptoms of their primary illnesses. This points to a significant number of "closet abusers and addicts" overlooked by treatment professionals. Unless professionals seek education regarding addictive disorders, clients will continue to mask symptoms, perpetuating addiction and exacerbating identified conditions. When clients challenge material related to addiction, remind them that even if they do not suffer from this malady, someone in their circle of family, friends, and acquaintances does. Understanding the addictive process, and the steps necessary to avoid entrapment, improves relationships and safeguards emotional well-being.

The feasibility of offering this program in a couples format is another treatment option explored during my workshops. My clinic offers multifamily group therapy; therefore, spouses do not attend client training groups. When leading multifamily groups, I incorporate materials from the training program into each session, paying special attention to communication skills, resolving resentments, and stress management. Clients and their significant others practice these skills in group, transfer them to the personal front, and report results in subsequent sessions. Opportunities to receive feedback from other families is a highlight of the family application concept. The reintroduction of materials initially presented in the training program provides clients with a review and additional practice time to master techniques.

Offering the program to families and couples in its original form is an additional option. Recommended modifications include the following:

1. Provide anger management-relapse prevention journals to clients *and* their significant others. Modify the family version to target enabling behaviors and subsequent physical and behavioral reactions.
2. Emphasize skills application using role plays, role reversal, and group feedback to motivate behavior change.
3. Assign practice scenarios specific to each client constellation for application outside group. Conduct follow-up reviews and apply modifications, if needed, during subsequent group sessions.
4. Target system behaviors in addition to individual behaviors for change.

Occasionally, I am asked to address the practicability of applying the program to women's groups. My response is that the program can be conducted without gender bias since both men and women experience addiction and anger. Women participating in my program report equal success in applying program materials. However, they desire a separate women's group since they are a minority in my clinic. Many feel restricted in their ability to openly address sensitive issues in the presence of men. This brings us to yet another issue: Can mixed groups of nonrelated clients generate positive results?

My contention is that mixed training groups *can* succeed, and even enhance the therapeutic process, if the therapist follows certain guidelines. Ideally, a symmetrical distribution of the sexes creates opportunities for heightened awareness regarding gender differences in the expression of feelings and needs. This information, carried into personal relationships, promotes positive interaction and system-focused recovery. Clients in mixed groups need encouragement to overcome animosities and work cooperatively toward common goals. The use of male-female therapeutic teams provides clients with appropriate models after which to pattern their own behavior. An added benefit for professionals is that cotherapy teams reduce splitting and gender-specific attacks on therapists, which occur more often in groups facilitated by a single therapist.

A final frontier before concluding this chapter involves application of the program to child and adolescent groups. With age-appropriate modifications, it is suitable for both client populations. When working with children between the ages of 5 and 12, primary considerations include attention span and concept formation. The younger the child, the shorter and more simplistic the presentation. The use of props—toys, puppets, paper and crayons—enhances leader effectiveness. Concepts must be presented in small chunks, with frequent repetition to promote skills acquisition. Finally, materials need redefinition, both in style and presentation, to facilitate behavior change.

Application of the program to adolescent groups requires great patience and skill. Adolescents are similar to addicts and alcoholics in their defiant, provocative reactions to suggestions for change. The projection of blame onto others is a standard response, and group leaders hold the dubious position of enemy or Pollyanna. The initial task involves gaining trust. Failure to accomplish this task dooms all future interventions. One strategy for overcoming animosity originates from the philosophy of going with rather than against resistance. An analogy from my childhood helps illustrate this concept.

When I was 12, I owned a spirited quarter horse mare. This horse had her own ideas about who was master. Each day at feeding time I walked into her pasture and attempted to corral her for feeding and grooming. Her response was to run, for hours, until we both reached a state of exhaustion. One day I decided to experiment. I walked into the pasture, but instead of chasing her, I sat in the grass with a feed bucket at my side. She snorted and galloped around me, attempting to elicit a response. I ignored her and continued to sit quietly. After several hours, she cautiously approached, allowing herself to be haltered. Thereafter, I never had need to chase her again. The moral is to let curiosity and time work in your favor. By avoiding power struggles, curiosity and peer pressure promote more active cooperation than any other intervention available.

A second strategy for overcoming mistrust is placement of youthful professionals in cotherapist roles. Assigning peer models to positions of authority lends credence to these positions (Egan, 1975; Potter-Efron, P., & Potter-Efron, 1991). Viewed as aligned with the needs and issues of teens, group members more readily accept models as "one of us." In ongoing groups, the use of long-term members serves the same purpose. These adolescents have already worked through resistance and trust the leader. They can actively confront inappropriate behaviors of new members without generating defensive reactions. Peer status affords credibility, further strengthening their persuasive powers. Finally, peer models provide examples of successful skills application in their own lives, encouraging newer members to seriously contemplate materials presented. Although peer models are not a panacea, their usefulness in adolescent groups merits consideration.

Part 4

Worksheets

WORKSHEET 1*

The Impact of Past Experiences on Current Life Choices

This worksheet is designed to assist you in exploring how role models and past experiences shaped and continue to influence your feelings, thoughts, and behavior. Although this exercise may uncover painful memories, the cleansing effect of releasing this material provides a foundation for the recovery process.

1. Who was your primary role model during childhood? ______

______

2. How did this role model express anger? ______

______

3. Did this person use alcohol or drugs to cope with feelings? YES _____ NO _____

______

4. What "messages" did you receive about sharing and expressing feelings and needs? (These messages include BOTH what they said AND what they did not say!) ______

5. Were these messages consistent or did actions and words contradict each other? ______

______

6. How did you feel as a child when you received messages from this person? ______

______

7. How do you feel as an adult when you look back on these messages and the way they have influenced your life? ____________________

____

8. What similarities and differences do you see in yourself and this person in the way feelings and needs are expressed? ____________________

____

9. If you had the power to "Change" the messages that guide your life choices, how would you rewrite them?

Old Message ____________________
New Message ____________________
Old Message ____________________
New Message ____________________
Old Message ____________________
New Message ____________________

10. Do you believe you CAN change your thoughts and behavior? YES _____ NO _____
If NO, what would it take for you to believe that change is possible? ____________________

____

11. What action can you take to initiate this process? ____________________

____

____

THANK YOU FOR PARTICIPATING IN THIS REVIEW OF THE PAST!

WORKSHEET 2*

Identification of Triggers and Cues

This worksheet is designed to help you identify triggers and cues that activate the anger-relapse cycle. Please complete each section to the best of your ability. Once completed, we will review this exercise as a group.

1. **Physical Cues** of Anger and Relapse: How does your body FEEL when you become angry or approach relapse? Do you notice certain muscles tensing? Does your heart beat faster? Do you experience cravings? Take a minute and think back to a recent episode when you were at risk. Please identify the *physical cues* you experienced and, if possible, list them in the order they appeared.

   Physical cue #1: ______________________________

   Physical cue #2: ______________________________

   Physical cue #3: ______________________________

2. **Emotional Cues** of Anger and Relapse: What EMOTIONS do you experience when you become angry or approach relapse? Do you feel anxious or confused? Are you excited or scared? Think of a recent episode when you were at risk. Please identify the emotional cues you experienced and, if possible, list them in the order they appeared.

   Emotional cue #1: ______________________________

   Emotional cue #2: ______________________________

   Emotional cue #3: ______________________________

3. **Cognitive Cues** of Anger and Relapse: What thoughts run through your mind when you become angry or approach relapse? Do you give yourself permission to act out, withdraw, or drink or use drugs because you DESERVE to get angry/high? Do you justify your behavior by telling yourself it's beyond your control, or someone else is to blame? Take a minute and think back to a recent episode when you were at risk. Please identify the cognitive cues you experienced and, if possible, list them in the order they appeared.

   Cognitive cue #1: ______________________

   Cognitive cue #2: ______________________

   Cognitive cue #3: ______________________

4. **Behavioral Cues** of Anger and Relapse: How do you BEHAVE when you become angry or approach relapse? Do you get pushy or demanding? Are you defensive? Do you withdraw and pout? Are you a pacer or a fist clencher? Think about a recent experience where you felt angry or wanted to take a drink or use drugs. Please identify the behavioral cues you experienced and, if possible, identify them in the order they appeared.

   Behavioral cue #1: ______________________

   Behavioral cue #2: ______________________

   Behavioral cue #3: ______________________

5. **Environmental Factors** Influencing Anger and Relapse: For most of us, anger and relapse are triggered by our reactions to specific people, places, times, or events. In the spaces provided below, please identify environmental factors that threaten your recovery.

   People: ______________________

   ____

Worksheet 2 (continued)

Places: ______________________________

____

Times: ______________________________

____

Events: ______________________________

____

6. Creating Your **Early Warning System:** Review your answers from the first four sections of this exercise. Try to identify when physical, emotional, cognitive, and behavioral reactions occurred and the order in which they appeared. How do you REACT PHYSICALLY, FEEL, THINK, and BEHAVE as your anger and relapse potential increases? Now look at the answers you gave in section 5. These factors are important, since they create reactions that may lead to inappropriate expressions of anger or to substance abuse. In the space provided below, identify ONE example of a high-risk situation and answer the remaining questions referring to that high-risk situation.

a. Define the high-risk situation. ______________________________

____

b. Where are you and who are you with? ______________________________

____

c. What time of day and what day of the week is it? ______________________________

____

d. What is occurring around you? ______________________________

____

e. How is your body reacting (physical signs)? ______

f. How are you FEELING (happy, sad, angry, scared, confused)? ______

g. What are you THINKING? ______

h. How are you BEHAVING? (List behaviors you are exhibiting.) ______

i. What can you do to alter the outcome of this event? ______

* Adapted from *Learning to live without violence: A handbook for men*. Copyright © 1982, 1985 by Daniel Jay Sonkin and Michael Durphy, Volcano Press, Volcano, California. Permission granted by Volcano Press.

WORKSHEET 3*

The Anger Management-Relapse Prevention Journal

The anger management-relapse prevention journal is designed to help you identify and track current patterns of feeling, thinking, and behavior across time. Daily entries are suggested to get the most benefit from your journal. Use the attached worksheets to document cues and reactions when you feel yourself becoming angry or at risk for relapse. Include the following information:

1. Day of the week, time of day, and date. This is important because it pinpoints times that are especially difficult.

2. What physical, emotional, cognitive, and behavioral cues alerted you that anger or relapse risks were increasing? Remember this pertains to what you FEEL inside—your EMOTIONAL STATE, your THOUGHTS—and how you BEHAVE. Also remember to note the order in which these signs appear.

3. Describe the situation that occurred IMMEDIATELY before you felt your anger or relapse risk increasing. Remember to include the following:

a. Whom you were with: ____________________

b. Where you were: ____________________

c. What you were doing: ____________________

4. How intense was your anger reaction or urge to use substances?

Mild _____ Moderate _____ Strong _____ Very Strong _____ Overpowering _____

5. What steps did you take to cope with your anger or urges to use substances?

____

____

6. Were you satisfied with your response? YES _____ NO _____

7. If you answered NO to question 6, what would you do differently next time you face a similar situation?

____

____

Remember to use the journal on a regular basis. Bedtime is a good time to take a few minutes and fill in your worksheets. When you run out of worksheets, ask me for more.

* Adapted from *Learning to live without violence: A handbook for men.* Copyright © 1982, 1985 by Daniel Jay Sonkin and Michael Durphy, Volcano Press, Volcano, California. Permission granted by Volcano Press.

Worksheet 3 (continued)

The Anger Management-Relapse Prevention Journal
Daily Worksheet

Date: ________ Time of Day: ________ Day of the Week: ______________

Signs of Escalating Anger or Relapse

Physical Signs:	Emotional Signs:
____________________	____________________
____________________	____________________
____________________	____________________

Cognitive Signs:	Behavioral Signs:
____________________	____________________
____________________	____________________
____________________	____________________

1. Describe the situation that occurred IMMEDIATELY before you noticed your anger or relapse potential increasing: ____________________

____

2. How intense was your anger reaction or urge to use substances?

Mild _____ Moderate _____ Strong _____ Very Strong _____ Overpowering _____

3. What steps did you take to cope with your anger or urge to use? ____________________

____

4. Were you satisfied with your response?

YES _____ NO _____

If NO, what would you do differently next time you face a similar situation? ____________________

____

____

WORKSHEET 4

Assessing Irrational Beliefs

This exercise is designed to help you identify irrational beliefs that increase your relapse potential. Please complete this worksheet to the best of your ability, and we will discuss your discoveries in group.

Common irrational beliefs that lead recovering alcoholics and addicts to relapse include the following:

- "I already slipped, so I might as well keep on drinking."
- "It's too late to change. I'm doomed to be this way forever."
- "My life is so stressful I deserve a drink/fix."
- "When I get angry the only thing I can do to make myself feel better is drink/use drugs."
- "I don't deserve to have a better life after what I've done."
- "What if I change and nobody else is willing to?"

Some of these irrational beliefs may be familiar to you. Please make a list of other messages that have contributed to relapse episodes in the past.

1. ____________________
2. ____________________
3. ____________________
4. ____________________

5. ______________________________

6. ______________________________

QUESTION: What do you get out of holding on to these faulty beliefs?

____

____

____

QUESTION: What are you willing to do to change them?

____

____

____

WORKSHEET 5*

Steps in the Problem-Solving Model

The problem-solving model promotes conflict resolution. Individuals learn to present feelings and needs clearly, without resorting to accusations or defensiveness. Below is a list of the building blocks essential for successful application of this model:

1. *Problem definition*. Be very specific in defining the problem. Address only one problem at a time. Start with smaller issues first. Larger issues can be tackled as you develop skill in applying the model.
2. *List ALL possible solutions*. Have participants brainstorm to generate possible solutions for the problem. Ideas should be listed without making judgments about whether they are "good" or "bad."
3. *Discuss each possible solution*. Review the advantages and disadvantages of each potential solution.
4. *Choose the best solution or combination of solutions.* Select the most effective means of resolving the problem with the least amount of sacrifice for *all* parties involved.
5. *Develop a plan of action*. Use this plan to implement the solution.
   - **a.** What steps are necessary to enact the plan?
   - **b.** When will the plan start? When will it end? (Target dates)
   - **c.** If more than one person is involved, what tasks are assigned to whom?

- **d.** Do you possess or have access to the necessary resources, skills, and energy to mobilize the plan?
- **e.** How will you measure whether the plan is working?

6. *Review and praise ALL efforts*. Recognize that change is *gradual* and new behaviors take time to establish. Concentrate on improvement, NOT perfection. PRAISE ALL EFFORTS, REGARDLESS OF THE OUTCOME!

7. *Identify problem areas for additional action.* When plans fail to yield intended results, analyze roadblocks that prevented the original plan from succeeding. Develop modifications and restate target dates and goals. Above all else—DON'T GIVE UP!

WE WILL PRACTICE THESE STEPS IN GROUP,
SO BE PREPARED TO PROVIDE EXAMPLES!

*Adapted from materials provided during a mediator training program conducted by the Alternative Dispute Resolution Center of Houston, 301 San Jacinto Street, Houston, Texas 77038.

WORKSHEET 6

Application of Communication Styles

This worksheet is designed to stimulate your thinking. We will review potential conflict situations and select communication styles to best resolve disharmony. Please participate freely—there are no wrong answers!

1. You are in the bank at closing time and someone cuts in line in front of you. There is only time for the teller to serve one more customer and you need the money to pay your rent tonight. What is the MOST APPROPRIATE RESPONSE? ______________________________

   Under what circumstances would you refrain from initiating the above response? ______________________________

2. You are walking your dog after dark and are confronted by a robber. This person demands your money and threatens violence if you refuse. (This person has a gun.) The BEST response would be ______________________________

   If despite this approach the robber becomes aggressive, other strategies to consider include ______________________________

   What factors should be considered before initiating these responses? ______________________________

3. Your significant other is determined to pick a fight. The issue is an old one that has been rehashed numerous times. Your FIRST response might be ______________________________

____

Other potential responses include ______________________________

____

4. Combative behavior is one of the four basic communication styles.

Is there ever a time when this approach would be your FIRST response choice? If so, when? __________

____

5. You are in a restaurant and accidentally bump into someone coming out of the restroom. You apologize and return to your table. The other person follows you and becomes verbally abusive. Your BEST RESPONSE is ______________________________

____

Other options might include ______________________________

____

WORKSHEET 6

Answer Key

1. The MOST APPROPRIATE RESPONSE would be to emphatically state, "Excuse me, you must not have seen me standing here. The end of the line is behind me."

   You WOULD NOT initiate this response if:

   a. The person is under the influence of a mind-altering substance.
   b. The person is agitated or becomes abusive.
   c. The person is retarded or mentally ill.

2. The BEST RESPONSE is to assume an acquiescent posture and offer no resistance to the robbery. Break eye contact, speak softly, and assure the robber you have no desire for a confrontation. If despite this approach the robber's aggressive behavior escalates:

   a. Yell fire and run toward a populated area.
   b. Assume a passive stance and wait until an opportunity appears to initiate defensive action.

   Factors to consider BEFORE initiating these responses include:

   a. The risk of injury if you initiate a defensive response.
   b. The odds of successful escape without being gunned down.

3. Your FIRST RESPONSE might be an empathic statement about the current situation. Other possible action includes:
   - **a.** Time-out to cool off and develop a constructive response.
   - **b.** Following time-out, problem solve the issue to identify strategies for successful resolution.

4. Combative behavior would be your FIRST response choice ONLY in situations where you must take defensive action to prevent injury or death.

5. Your BEST RESPONSE would be to *again* acknowledge responsibility for the mishap. If conflict escalates despite efforts to defuse it, other options include:
   - **a.** Assume an acquiescent posture (i.e., break eye contact and use a soft, monotone voice and relaxed body position); allow the other person to express feelings until they cool off.
   - **b.** Ask the person to return to his or her table, explaining that you have apologized and feel no further interaction is needed.
   - **c.** Approach the manager, explain the situation, and request third-party assistance.

The Worksheet 6 exercise elicits a variety of reactions among participants. Many become angry when acquiescent or empathic responses are suggested. Common complaints include the following:

- "Jo! Do you really expect for me to allow that _______ to treat me that way?"
- "Are you totally nuts? If I let it happen once, I'll be a victim for the rest of my life!"
- "The only way to handle someone like that is to beat the_______ out of them!"
- "You NEVER walk away—NEVER!"

WORKSHEET 7

Asking for What You Want and Learning to Say No

Many times we fail to express true feelings when facing situations that require us to make or decline requests. This exercise is designed to help you become more aware of your reactions and the factors that motivate them.

Instructions

Review the list of factors that interfere with effective communication. Which of these factors are present in your life? Think of a person you have difficulty saying no to or asking for something you need. Answer the following questions with this person in mind and be prepared to process the exercise in group.

1. Identify the person you have difficulty sharing feelings with (provide his or her name and relationship to you)

   ____

2. Identify the roadblocks to communication that prevent you from sharing feelings honestly with this individual:

   a. ____________________ d. ____________________

   b. ____________________ e. ____________________

   c. ____________________ f. ____________________

3. What have you always wanted to ask this person for but haven't?

What prevented you from asking?

4. When this person asked you to ______ you wish you had said NO but didn't. The reason you were unable to decline is ______

5. What you hope to do differently in future interactions with this person is ______

6. What do you think this person's reaction would be? ______

SESSION 9

Asking for What You Want and Learning to Say No (Client Handout)

Guidelines for Making Requests

1. Clearly state your request using "I" statements: "I would like . . . ," "I want or need. . . ."
2. Avoid language that is demanding or hostile: "You should"; "You have to"; "I expect"; "If you don't I'll. . . ."
3. Be prepared to receive no's to some of your requests. Remember, other people have the right to say yes or no, just as you do! Remember that if the response is no, it frees you to explore other options.

Guidelines for Declining Requests.

1. Clearly state your response: "No, I can't ________________________."
2. Realize that although you may want to provide an explanation, you are under no obligation to do so.
3. Avoid becoming defensive or hostile. Remember that you have the **right** to say no.
4. If the other person refuses to take no for an answer, do not feel obligated to argue your position! If you feel yourself becoming angry, take a time-out! This may prevent a relapse!

Homework Assignment

Using the exercise we completed in group today as a guide, if possible, practice making and declining requests with the person you identified on your worksheet. **Hint:** Start with small issues that will not lead to major shifts in the relationship. Gradually apply assertive responses to more important issues as you gain skill in using this new form of communication. Be patient if you don't get immediate results. Remember that change requires adjustment not only for ourselves, but also for the people we interact with on a day-to-day basis.

WORKSHEET 8*

Assessment of Response Choices

This worksheet is designed to assess the strategies you currently use to manage stress. Please place an **X** beside each statement that is true for you. Once you have completed the worksheet, we will practice replacing negative strategies with alternative interventions.

Positive Stress Management Strategies

When experiencing stress, which of the following activities do you use to resolve it?

1. Listen to music ______
2. Watch TV or go to the movies ______
3. Read a book or magazine ______
4. Write in a journal or diary ______
5. Exercise, walk, or jog ______
6. Redirect your activity ______
7. Take a short nap ______
8. Practice meditation or deep breathing ______
9. Visit or call a friend ______
10. Do a good deed for someone ______
11. Take a shower or bath ______
12. Openly express feelings ______
13. Take time-out to think about options ______
14. Other: ______
15. Other: ______

Negative Stress Management Strategies

When experiencing stress, which of the following activities do you use to escape?

1. Avoid social contact with others ______
2. Anticipate the worst possible outcome ______
3. Think about the possibility of suicide ______
4. Smoke tobacco ______
5. Overeat, eat junk food, skip meals ______
6. Use alcohol or other drugs ______
7. Become irritable or use abusive language ______
8. Drink excessive amounts of coffee ______
9. Spend money you don't have to spare ______
10. Sit and feel sorry for yourself ______
11. Blame others for your problems ______
12. Drive fast and recklessly ______
13. Sleep as an escape ______
14. Other: ______
15. Other: ______

A. How many NEGATIVE strategies did you list? ____________________

B. How many POSITIVE strategies did you list? ____________________

C. If you listed more negative than positive responses, what steps could you take to change this pattern?

____

____

*Adapted, with permission of the publisher, from: Munz, D. (1983). *Stress management participant's manual.* St. Louis: St. Louis University Medical Center—Healthline.

WORKSHEET 9

Assessing Personal Resentments

This worksheet will help you identify and work through personal resentments affecting your recovery. Please answer the following questions, and be prepared to share your responses in group.

1. What is your greatest personal resentment?

____

____

2. What person(s) does this resentment involve? (Remember, resentments can be directed toward yourself.)

____

3. How long have you held this resentment? ____________________

4. Have you attempted to resolve it? YES _____ NO _____

If your answer was YES, please explain: ____________________

____

5. If the resentment is unresolved, what negative consequences has it created?

____

____

What secondary gains have you realized?

____

____

6. Having completed this exercise, can you think of alternative strategies you might use to resolve the resentment? YES ____ NO ____

If you answered YES, what action can you take?

____

____

Epilogue

As I write this epilogue for my first book, the feeling most present is an overwhelming sense of relief! After years of carrying these thoughts and ideas inside my head, I FINALLY committed them to paper! If I have challenged your thinking, stimulated your creativity, or helped you empower a single client, I achieved my intended result. Teaching clients to take risks, fail, and try again is the greatest gift a therapist can offer. By helping them discover the beauty of being human, we set them free from the guilt and shame that perpetuates the cycle of anger, addiction, and relapse. If we do our job well, they depart with the necessary skills to successfully move beyond treatment into recovery. As my good friend Bo Cook says, "This is treatment, out there is recovery—go live it!" In closing, I leave you with these final thoughts:

1. Anger and addiction have many common qualities. Some are amenable to change, some are not. Our responsibility is to inspire our clients to set realistic goals and strive to achieve them, because of rather than in spite of whom they are.
2. Anger and addiction potentiate each other's negative effects. Teaching clients to recognize the relationship between these powerful forces is the first step in a process called recovery.

3. Identifying triggers that elicit negative responses is a critical element of skills training. Remember the rattlesnake analogy: Awareness of an event's meaning precedes the ability to determine how best to respond.
4. Participation in the anger management-relapse prevention training program is the first step in a lifelong process of acquiring, reviewing, and modifying thoughts and behaviors. Much like a freshly cut lawn, outward appearances of perfection soon become unkempt if not tended regularly.
5. As a therapist, you will experience many "failures" and few successes. Reframe each "failure" so it becomes a process of shaping cognitive and behavior change. Regardless of whether we have the privilege of observing the outcome of a client's experience, the knowledge imparted during treatment becomes permanently imprinted in their psyches. If we produce a single crack in the wall called denial, recovery remains a possibility. Remember, small cracks often serve as catalysts for future change.
6. Finally, practice what you teach! The most effective teachers are those willing to experience that which they ask of their students. This training program works for my clients and it works for me. I hope it works for you!

References

Abramson, L., Seligman, M., & Teasdale, J. (1978). Learned helplessness in humans: Critique and reformulation. *Journal of Abnormal Psychology, 87*, 49–74.

Annis, H. (1986). A relapse prevention model for treatment of alcoholics. In W. Miller & N. Heather (Eds.), *Treating addictive behaviors: Processes of change* (pp. 407–433). New York: Plenum.

Annis, H., & Davis, C. (1987a). Assessment of expectancies in alcohol dependent clients. In G. A. Marlatt & D. Donovan (Eds.), *Assessment of addictive behaviors* (pp. 84–111). New York: Guilford Press.

Annis, H., & Davis, C. (1987b). Self-efficacy and the prevention of alcoholic relapse: Initial findings from a treatment trial. In T. Baker & D. Cannon (Eds.), *Addictive disorders: Psychological research on assessment and treatment* (pp. 88–112). New York: Praeger.

Anonymous (1976), *Alcoholics anonymous: The story of how many thousands of men and women have recovered from alcoholism* (3rd ed.). New York: Alcoholics Anonymous World Services.

Bandura, A. (1969). *Principles of behavior modification*. New York: Holt, Rinehart & Winston.

Bandura, A. (Ed.). (1971a). *Psychological modeling: Conflict theories*. Chicago: Aldine-Atherton.

Bandura, A. (1971b). Psychotherapy based upon modeling principles. In A. E. Bergin & S. L. Garfield (Eds.), *Handbook of psychotherapy and behavior change* (pp. 653–708). New York: Wiley.

Bandura, A. (1974). Behavior therapy and the models of man. *American Psychologist, 29*, 859–869.

Bandura, A. (1977). *Social learning theory*. Englewood Cliffs, NJ: Prentice-Hall.

Bandura, A. (1986). *Social foundations of thought and action: A social-cognitive theory*. Englewood Cliffs, NJ: Prentice-Hall.

Barlow, D. H. (1978). Aversive procedures. In W. S. Agras (Ed.), *Behavior modification: Principles and clinical applications* (2nd ed., pp. 87–125). Boston: Little, Brown.

Beck, A. (1988). *Love is never enough*. New York: Harper & Row.

Beck, A., Rush, A. J., Shaw, B., & Emery, G. (1979). *Cognitive therapy of depression*. New York: Guilford.

Beck, A. T. (1976). *Cognitive therapy and emotional disorders*. New York: International Universities Press.

Beck, A. T. (1987). Cognitive therapy. In J. K. Zeig (Ed.), *The evolution of psychotherapy* (pp. 149–178). New York: Brunner/Mazel.

Bellack, A. S., & Hersen, M. (Eds.). (1985). *Dictionary of behavior therapy techniques*. New York: Pergamon.

Black, C., & Bucky, S. (1986). Interpersonal and emotional consequences of being an adult child of an alcoholic. *International Journal of the Addictions*, *21*(2), 213–231.

Bootzin, R. (1980). *Abnormal psychology* (3rd ed.). New York: Random House.

Corey, G. (1991). Theory and practice of counseling and psychotherapy (4th ed.). Pacific Grove, CA: Brooks/Cole.

Daley, D. (1988). *Relapse prevention*. Bradenton, FL: Human Services Institute.

Davis, J. (1984). Endorphins: New waves in brain chemistry. Garden City, NY: Doubleday.

DeRubeis, R. J., & Beck, A. T. (1988). Cognitive therapy. In K. S. Dobson (Ed.), *Handbook of cognitive-behavioral therapies* (4th ed., pp. 273–306). New York: Guilford Press.

Deschner, J. (1984). *How to end the hitting habit: Anger control for battering couples*. New York: Free Press.

DiClemente, C. C. (1993). Changing addictive behaviors: A process perspective. *Current Directions in Psychological Science*, *2*(4), 101–106.

Egan, G. (1975). *The skilled helper*. Monterey, CA: Brooks/Cole.

Ellis, A. (1962). *Reason and emotion in psychotherapy*. New York: Lyle Stuart.

Ellis, A. (1971). *Growth through reason*. Hollywood, CA: Wilshire Books.

Ellis, A. (1973). *Humanistic psychotherapy*. New York: McGraw-Hill.

Ellis, A. (1977). Fun in psychotherapy. *Rational Living, 12*(1), 2–6.

Ellis, A. (1985). *Overcoming resistance: Rational-emotive therapy with difficult clients*. New York: Springer.

Ellis, A. (1987a). The evolution of rational-emotive therapy (RET) and cognitive behavioral therapy (CBT). In J. K. Zeig (Ed.), *The evolution of psychotherapy* (pp. 107–132). New York: Brunner/Mazel.

Ellis, A. (1987b). The use of rational humorous songs in psychotherapy. In W. F. Fry, Jr., & W. A. Salemeh (Eds.), *Handbook of humor and psychotherapy* (pp. 265–287). Sarasota, FL: Professional Resource Exchange.

Ellis, A. (1988). *How to stubbornly refuse to make yourself miserable about anything—yes anything!* Secaucus, NJ: Lyle Stuart.

Ellis, A., & Becker, I. (1982). *A guide to personal happiness*. North Hollywood, CA: Wilshire.

Ellis, A., & Bernard, M. E. (Eds.). (1984). *Rational-emotive approaches to the problems of childhood*. New York: Plenum.

Ellis, A., & Bernard, M. E. (Eds.). (1985). *Clinical applications of rational-emotive therapy*. New York: Plenum.

Ellis, A., & Dryden, W. (1987). *The practice of rational-emotive therapy*. New York: Springer.

Ellis, A., & Greiger, R. (Eds.). (1977). *Handbook of rational-emotive therapy*. New York: Springer.

Ellis, A., & Greiger, R. (Eds.). (1986). *Handbook of rational-emotive therapy* (Vols. 1–2). New York: Springer.

Ellis, A., & Harper, R. A. (1975). *A new guide to rational living*. North Hollywood, CA: Wilshire.

Ellis, A., McInerney, J., DiGiuseppe, R., & Yeager, R. (1988). *Rational-emotive therapy with alcoholics and substance abusers*. New York: Pergamon.

Ellis, A., & Whiteley, J. M. (Eds). (1979). *Theoretical and empirical foundations of rational-emotive therapy*. Monterey, CA: Brooks/Cole.

Fonberg, E. (1979). Physiological mechanisms of emotional and instrumental aggression. In S. Feshback & A. Fraczek (Eds.), *Aggression and behavior change: Biological and social processes* (pp. 6–53). New York: Praeger.

Gorski, T., & Miller, M. (1986). *Staying sober: A guide for relapse prevention*. Independence, MO: Independence Press.

Green, E., & Green, E. (1979). General and specific applications of thermal feedback. In J. V. Basmajian (Ed.), *Biofeedback: Principles and practice for clinicians* (pp. 153–169). Baltimore: Williams & Williams.

Hecker, M., & Lunde, D. (1985). On the diagnosis and treatment of chronically hostile individuals. In M. Chesney & R. Rosenman (Eds.), *Anger and hostility in cardiovascular and behavioral disorders* (pp. 227–240). New York: Hemisphere.

Jellinek, E. M. (1960). *The disease concept of alcoholism*. New Haven, CT: Hillhouse Press.

Ketcham, K. & Mueller, L. A. (1985), *Eating right to live sober*. Rotan, TX: Madrona.

Leeper, R. W. (1968). The motivational theory of emotion. In M. B. Arnold (Ed.), *The nature of emotion*. Baltimore: Penguin.

Leiber, C. S., Hasumara, Y., Teschke, R., Matsuzaki, S., & Korsten, M. (1975). The effect of chronic ethanol consumption on acetaldehyde metabolism. In K. O. Lindros & C. J. P. Ericksson (Eds.), *The role of acetaldehyde in the actions of ethanol*. Helsinki: Finnish Foundation for Alcohol Studies (23).

MaClean, P. D. (1955). The limbic system. *Psychosomatic Medicine*, *17*, 355.

Mahoney, M. J. (1974). *Cognition and behavior modification*. Cambridge, MA: Ballinger.

Mahoney, M. J., & Thoresen, C. E. (1974). *Self-control : Power to the person*. Monterey, CA: Brooks/Cole.

Maier, S., Seligman, M., & Solomon, R. (1969). Pavlovian fear conditioning and learned helplessness. In B. A. Campbell & R. M. Church (Eds.), *Punishment* (pp. 299–342). New York: Appleton-Century-Crofts.

Marlatt, G. A., & George, W. H. (1984). Relapse prevention: An introduction and overview of the model. *British Journal of the Addictions*, *79*(3), 261–273.

Marlatt, G., & Gordon, J. (Eds.). (1985). *Relapse prevention: A self-control strategy for the maintenance of behavior change*. New York: Guilford Press.

Meichenbaum, D. (1977). *Cognitive behavior modification: An integrative approach*. New York: Plenum.

Meichenbaum, D. (1986). Cognitive behavior modification. In F. H. Kanfer & A. P. Goldstein (Eds.), *Helping people change: A textbook of methods* (pp. 346–380). New York: Pergamon Press.

Mello, N. K. (1972). Behavioral studies in alcoholism. In B. Kissin & H. Begleiter (Eds.), *The biology of alcoholism* (Vol. 2, pp. 219–291). New York: Plenum.

Milam, J., & Ketcham, K. (1981). *Under the influence: A guide to the myths and realities of alcoholism.* Seattle: Madrona.

Miller, M., Gorski, T., & Miller, D. K. (1982). *Learning to live again—A guide to recovery from alcoholism.* Independence, MO: Independence Press.

Moyer, K. E. (1976). Kinds of aggression and their physiological basis. In K. E. Moyer (Ed.), *Physiology of aggression and implications for control: An anthology of readings* (pp. 1–21). New York: Raven.

Mueller, A., & Ketcham, K. (1987). *Recovering: How to get and stay sober.* Toronto: Bantam Books.

Munz, D. (1983). *Stress management participant's manual.* St. Louis: St. Louis University Medical Center—Healthline.

Nathan, P. E., Titler, N. A., Lowenstein, L. M., Solomon, P., & Rossi, A. M. (1970). Behavioral analysis on chronic alcoholism. *Archives of General Psychiatry, 22,* 419–430.

Patterson, G. R. (1985). A microsocial analysis of anger and irritable behavior. In M. Chesney & R. Rosenman (Eds.), *Anger and hostility in cardiovascular and behavioral disorders* (pp. 83–100). New York: Hemisphere.

Potter-Efron, P., & Potter-Efron, R. (1991). Anger as a treatment concern with alcoholics and affected family members. *Alcoholism Treatment Quarterly, 8*(3).

Potter-Efron, R. (1989). *Shame, guilt, and alcoholism: Treatment issues in clinical practice.* New York: Haworth Press.

Potter-Efron, R. (1990). Differential diagnosis of physiological, psychiatric, and sociocultural conditioning associated with aggression and substance abuse. In R. Potter-Efron & P. Potter-Efron (Eds.), *Aggression, family violence, and chemical dependency* (pp. 37–50). New York: Haworth Press.

Potter-Efron, R., & Potter-Efron, P. (1989). *Letting go of shame: Understanding shame in our lives.* Center City, MN: Hazeldon/ Harper & Row.

Potter-Efron, R., & Potter-Efron, P. (1991a). *Anger, alcoholism, and addiction: Treating individuals, couples, and families.* New York: W. W. Norton.

Potter-Efron, R., & Potter-Efron, P. (1991b). *Ending our resentments.* Center City, MN: Hazeldon Press.

Rogers, C. (1951). *Client centered therapy.* Boston: Houghton Mifflin.

Rogers, C., & Wood, J. (1974). Client centered theory: Carl Rogers. In A. Burton (Ed.), *Operational theories of personality.* New York: Brunner/Mazel.

Schachter, J. (1957). Pain, fear, and anger in hypertensives and normotensives. *Psychosomatic Medicine, 19,* 17–29.

Schachter, S. (1971). *Emotion, obesity, and crime.* New York: Academic Press.

Seligman, M. (1975). *Helplessness: On depression, development, and death.* San Francisco: Freeman.

Seyle, H. (1956). *The stress of life.* New York: McGraw-Hill.

Seyle, H. (1974). *Stress without distress.* Philadelphia: Lippincott.

Schuckit, M. A., Li, T. K., Cloninger, C. R., & Deitrich, R. A. (1985). The genetics of alcoholism: A summary of the proceedings of the conference convened at the University of California, Davis. *Alcoholism: Clinical and Experimental Research, 9*(6), 475–492.

Shapiro, D. (1965). *Neurotic styles.* New York: Basic Books.

Skinner, B. F. (1948). *Walden II.* New York: Macmillan.

Skinner, B. F. (1971). *Beyond freedom and dignity*. New York: Knopf.

Smedes, L. (1984). *Forgive and forget*. New York: Pocket Books.

Sonkin, J., & Durphy, M. (1985). *Learning to live without violence: A handbook for men* (rev. ed.). San Francisco: Volcano Press.

Spielberger, C. (1988). *State-trait anger expression inventory: Research edition*. Odessa, FL: Psychological Assessment Resources.

Spielberger, C., Jacobs, G., Russell, S., & Crane, R. S. (1983). Assessment of anger: The state-trait anger scale. In J. Butcher & C. Spielberger (Eds.), *Advances in personality assessment* (Vol. 2, pp. 161–186). Hillsdale, NJ: Lawrence Erlbaum.

Spielberger, C., Krasner, S., & Solomon, E. (1988). The experience, expression, and control of anger. In M. Janisse (Ed.), *Health psychology: Individual differences and stress* (pp. 88–108). New York: Springer-Verlag.

Thoresen, C. E., & Coates, T. J. (1980). What does it mean to be a behavior therapist? In C. E. Thoresen (Ed.), *The behavior therapist*. Monterey, CA: Brooks/Cole.

Vaillant, G. E. (1983). *The natural history of alcoholism: Causes, patterns, and paths to recovery*. Cambridge, MA: Harvard University Press.

Walen, S. R., DiGuiseppe, R., & Wessler, R. L. (1980). *A practitioner's guide to rational-emotive therapy*. New York: Oxford University Press.

Walfish, S. (1990). Anxiety and anger among abusers of different substances. *Drug and Alcohol Dependence*, *25*(3), 253–256.

Walker, L. (1980). *The battered woman syndrome*. New York: Springer.

Wallace, J. (1985). *Alcoholism: New light on the disease*. Warwick, RI: Edgehill.

Wegscheider, S. (1981). *Another chance: Hope and health for the alcoholic family*. Palo Alto, CA: Science & Behavior Books.

Wegscheider-Cruse, S. (1976). *The family trap*. St. Paul: Nurturing Network.

Wessler, R. A., & Wessler, R. L. (1980). *The principles and practice of rational-emotive therapy*. San Francisco: Jossey-Bass.

Williams, R., & Williams, V. (1993). *Anger kills*. New York: Times Books.

Woititz, J. (1983). *Adult children of alcoholics*. Hollywood, FL: Health Communications.

Wolf, E. (1988). *Treating the self*. New York: Guilford Press.